The Wisdom of Swedish Death Cleaning

Unclutter Your Life to Find Meaning & Pur

By Steven Todd Bryant

Disclaimer

This book is not intended to be a substitute for the medical, legal, or financial advice of a licensed professional. Always consult your doctor, lawyer, and financial counselor before making any life changes. Although the author and publisher have made every effort to ensure the information in this book was correct at press time, the author and publisher do not assume and hereby disclaim any liability to any party for any loss, damage, or disruption caused by errors or omissions for any reason or from any damages suffered because of this publication. In some cases, stories have been fictionalized, and names and identifying details have been omitted or changed to protect the privacy of individuals.

Table of Contents

Introduction

My Brush with Death

The Seven Essential Steps of Swedish Death Cleaning

   Step 1. The Art of Swedish Death Cleaning: Keep, Donate,

   Sell, Recycle, or Trash

   Step 2. Share Your Legacy with Loved Ones

   Step 3. Digitize Old Photos, Documents & Memorabilia

   Step 4. Leave an Uncluttered Legacy: Finances, Will, &

   Funeral Plans

   Step 5. The Power of Simplicity and Minimalism

   Step 6. Everything is Temporary

   Step 7. Mindfulness, Accepting Reality, & Gratitude

Conclusion

Note from the Author

About the Author

Steven Todd Bryant is a best-selling author and crisis counselor and is the founder of ToxicFamily.org. He is best known for his international best-selling book "The Toxic Family Solution." He was on staff at the University of Southern California for two decades and holds a BA in Communications and an MA in Theological Studies.

Best-Selling Books by the Author

The Toxic Family Solution

The Wisdom of Swedish Death Cleaning

Dedication

Many thanks to William E. Range, MC, LMHC
Licensed Therapist, Port Townsend, WA

Introduction

Are you tired of living with a cluttered home, heart, mind, and soul? Do you long for a simpler, more fulfilling life? In today's fast-paced world, we often find ourselves surrounded by an overwhelming amount of stuff. Our consumer culture is so deeply ingrained in our society that it's easy to lose sight of what truly matters in life and who we truly are. We fill our lives with belongings, accumulating more and more, hoping they will bring us happiness and fulfillment. We are often disappointed when these items fail to meet our needs. After the initial rush of a new purchase fades, amidst all the clutter we have collected, we often feel disconnected, overwhelmed, and yearning for something deeper.

Swedish Death Cleaning, although it may initially sound

morbid, is deeply rooted in a profound wisdom with the power to change the way you live. When you declutter, organize, and simplify your physical space, you open the door to a more peaceful, spacious, organized, intentional, and fulfilling way of life. Concepts such as everything is temporary, gratitude, minimalism, mindfulness, and self-compassion allow self-reflection and personal growth to flourish. Suddenly, the person you were meant to be begins to emerge.

Your true self is constantly bombarded and distracted by advertisements urging you to acquire more, accumulate possessions, and chase after materialistic goals. In this fast-paced and cluttered world, it's no wonder many of us long for something deeper.

What if there was a different way to live your best life in the present moment? What if there was a way to break free from the false and unfulfilled promises of consumerism? Is there a path that can lead you toward a simpler, more organized, and more fulfilling life? Is there an uncluttered space where your mind can be clear and your heart can soar? Welcome to "The Wisdom of Swedish Death Cleaning: Unclutter Your Life to Find Meaning & Purpose."

In this transformative book, I invite you to embark on a journey of self-discovery and self-reflection. Drawing inspiration from the Scandinavian philosophy of Swedish Death Cleaning, we will explore how minimalism and mindfulness can benefit you in your daily life. This book explains these concepts in a clear, easy-to-understand and approachable manner. By embracing the wisdom of this unique approach, you will learn to let go of excess clutter and reclaim the life you were meant to live.

Uncluttering is not just about tidying up physical spaces; it's about freeing ourselves from the mental and emotional clutter that holds us back. By shedding unnecessary distractions, possessions, and commitments, we create space for what truly matters—the pursuit of authentic love, happiness, genuine connections, and a sense of purpose.

This book promises to guide you on a transformative journey, offering practical strategies and actionable steps to help you unclutter your life, both externally and internally. You will discover how to cultivate mindfulness, live in the present moment, and find profound meaning and purpose amidst the chaos of everyday life.

Together, we will explore the art of letting go, deconstructing the myth that material possessions equate to happiness. You will learn how to declutter your physical surroundings, simplify your daily routines, and cultivate a mindset that prioritizes experiences over possessions. This book starts out very practical and then dives deeply into the easy-to-grasp concepts of mindfulness and minimalism.

The path to living your best life begins with the choices you make today. Right here. Right now. You cannot continue to do the same things and expect a different outcome. If you want to change your life, you have to do something different. By embracing the principles of minimalism and mindfulness embedded in Swedish Death Cleaning, you will unlock the freedom to savor each moment, find joy in the simplest of pleasures, and discover a renewed sense of purpose and fulfillment.

So, if you're ready to embark on a transformative journey and learn how to unclutter your life to find meaning and purpose, let this book be your guide. Get ready to live intentionally, shed the unnecessary, and embrace a more conscious and fulfilling life that celebrates the present moment while unlocking the true essence of who you are.

In this extensive exploration of Swedish Death Cleaning, we will explore seven essential steps that will guide you on this transformative journey. These steps have been carefully identified to help you unburden yourself from the weight of excess possessions and emotional baggage. By following them, you will embark on a path toward freedom, simplicity, and a more intentional life.

Step 1: The Art of Swedish Death Cleaning: Keep, Donate, Sell, Recycle, or Trash

The first step in the process of Swedish Death Cleaning is to examine your possessions and measure their significance in your life. We often accumulate belongings without truly considering their impact on our lives. Every new thing we purchase consumes our own time, space, and energy. This step encourages you to assess each item and make a conscious decision about whether to keep, donate, sell, recycle, or discard it. By implementing this approach, you can gradually create a physical environment and space that aligns with your current values and priorities.

Step 2: Share Your Legacy with Loved Ones

We don't have to wait until the end of our lives to begin sharing our legacy with loved ones. When people pass away, cherished family heirlooms are often discarded because the family didn't fully understand their significance, value, or history. As you navigate the process of Swedish Death Cleaning, it becomes essential to consider the legacy you wish to leave behind. This step encourages you to share your stories, experiences, and wisdom with your loved ones. By engaging in open conversations and documenting your personal history, you can create lasting connections and ensure that your memories and life lessons live on.

Step 3: Digitize Old Photos, Documents & Memorabilia

Our lives are filled with photographs, documents, and memorabilia that hold significant meaning. However, these physical artifacts are susceptible to damage and decay over time. In this step, we explore the importance of digitizing these valuable pieces of our personal history. By preserving them in a digital format, you can safeguard their longevity and share them with future generations.

Step 4: Leave an Uncluttered Legacy: Finances, Will, & Funeral Plans

In addition to physical possessions, our financial matters and end-of-life plans also play a crucial role in Swedish Death Cleaning. Don't wait until it's too late to organize your finances, create a will, and make your funeral arrangements. Putting your life in order will ease the burden on your loved ones during a very difficult time. This step highlights the importance of preparing for the inevitable and embracing the peace of mind that comes with knowing your affairs are in order.

Step 5: The Power of Simplicity and Minimalism

Simplicity and minimalism lie at the heart of Swedish Death Cleaning. In this step, we explore the transformative power of embracing these principles in our lives. By intentionally cultivating an environment free from excessive distractions, we create space for what truly matters—relationships, experiences, and personal growth. Simplicity and minimalism enable us to focus on the essentials of life and find fulfillment in the beauty and simplicity of the present moment.

Step 6: Everything is Temporary

Everything in life is temporary. Everything in life has a birth and death cycle. We should not be surprised when relationships end, things change, or life offers us something different than we expected. Recognizing this impermanence is a central tenet of Swedish Death Cleaning. In this step, we explore the philosophy of embracing change and letting go of attachment. By understanding the temporary nature of our lives and everything around us, we can navigate life's challenges with resilience and find adventure and wonder in every moment.

Step 7: Mindfulness, Accepting Reality, & Gratitude

Mindfulness, acceptance, and gratitude are essential

components of Swedish Death Cleaning. This step emphasizes the importance of cultivating a present-centered mindset, accepting life's inevitable ups and downs, and practicing gratitude for what is. We can end suffering in our lives by merely accepting life as it is. When we argue with life or deny what is really happening, we experience pain. By integrating these practices into our daily lives, we can cultivate a deeper sense of meaning, purpose, happiness and joy.

Don't wait until it's too late to put off this transformational journey. The wisdom of Swedish Death Cleaning extends far beyond mere preparation for the end of life; it is an invitation to fully embrace the life you were meant to live today.

Don't miss the beauty life has for you. Every day is an opportunity to live a more abundant and meaningful adventure. Your best life begins today!

—Steven Todd Bryant

Note: The first four steps in this book are very how-to, focusing on the practical steps of the art of Swedish Death Cleaning. The second half of the book explores the philosophical wisdom and mindfulness inherent in this transformational process.

My Brush With Death

A brush with death jolted me awake. My doctor informed me that I might have prostate cancer, the same illness that claimed my father's life a few years ago. Confronting the possibility of my own mortality shook me to the core. While aimlessly flipping through television channels, I stumbled upon Amy Poehler's series showcasing Swedish Death Cleaning. In between doctor visits, I began to binge-watch the entire series. I laughed and cried and learned a lot about myself, my views on death, and all of the work I needed to do if I was going to leave an uncluttered legacy for my family.

I set out to learn all I could about Swedish Death Cleaning. After I learned the basic principles, I began to dive deep into the wisdom and philosophy behind this emerging trend. I began to focus on life-altering concepts such as minimalism, mindfulness, letting go of attachment, gratitude, and the impermanence of life.

As I began to practice the steps I was learning, I meditated on this life-changing wisdom. The principles of Swedish Death Cleaning presented a profound challenge to me—one that compelled me to confront my own mortality. It forced me to look deep within myself, posing vital questions about the way I approached life. Was I truly seizing every opportunity and unlocking my fullest potential? Had I discovered the meaning and purpose of my existence? Were my possessions distracting me from really living?

Let me start at the beginning. Shortly after completing my first book The Toxic Family Solution I began experiencing physical symptoms that signaled something was wrong. The pain I was enduring prompted me to undergo my annual PSA blood test earlier than scheduled. A PSA test is a prostate-specific blood test which can screen for cancer in the prostate. Previous years' results had been normal, providing no cause for concern. However, this time, the test produced startlingly different findings.

My doctor urgently summoned me to his office and delivered

the life-altering news. He informed me that there was a high possibility of prostate cancer, the same illness that had claimed my father's life a few years prior. While the doctor remained hopeful that we caught it early, he made it clear that prostate cancer posed a serious and potentially fatal threat to me, just as it did to my father. To rule out cancer, the doctor prescribed potent medication and antibiotics, hoping the blood test results indicated an infection instead of cancer. When I inquired about the steps I should take, he advised me to get my affairs in order, just in case.

Until that fateful day, the notion of my mortality had never truly crossed my mind. I attend church regularly and asked Jesus into my heart when I was a child. But the thought of dying ran contrary to my false belief that I would live forever. Upon receiving the blood test results, I was jolted awake.

Questions I had never fully considered filled my mind:

-What if I were to die suddenly?

-How would my family cope with the overwhelming task of sorting through the belongings I had accumulated throughout my lifetime?

-How much unnecessary clutter had I stored away or left untouched in closets and cabinets?

-How many items, forgotten and unused for decades, lurked

in the depths of my home?

-Were my finances in order?

-What type of funeral arrangements did I want?

After my father's death from prostate cancer, it was a challenging time for my mother. Having grown up during the Great Depression, he tended to be a bit of a hoarder, keeping almost everything. For example, my mom discovered dozens of old glass jars filled with rusty nails and wooden boxes filled with old tools, likely inherited from previous generations. With the help of her sister, they managed to sort through his belongings, but it was emotionally draining while still grieving his passing.

Observing my family bear the weight of this challenge, I resolved to spare them such burdens. I decided to adopt a fresh perspective on death. Instead of denying death's reality, I chose to embrace the wisdom of Swedish Death Cleaning as I contemplated my life and death. I vowed to take responsibility for organizing my legacy before my journey's end.

As part of this wake-up call, one of my first steps was confronting my consumerist lifestyle. I suddenly realized the suffocating grip materialism had on my life—countless hours of my precious life had been wasted in a never-ending cycle of dusting, maintaining, protecting, insuring, worrying about, organizing, and replacing possessions. Meanwhile, the true essence of my life slipped through my fingers unnoticed. The more things I had to procure, the less time I had to live my authentic life. Instead of truly living, I had become a caretaker of things.

After my first book was about to be published, I sold my house in Port Townsend, Washington, and moved to Seattle. I rented a spacious apartment downtown. Mindlessly, I packed all my belongings and hauled them halfway across the state to my new urban dwelling. But I didn't clean house. My closets were filled floor to ceiling with boxes of things I hadn't looked at in twenty years. At one point, I even considered renting a storage unit to reclaim much-needed square footage in my huge walk-in closet. But after doing the math, I realized that long-term storage was impractical and an expense I didn't need to incur.

After the doctor told me to get my affairs in order, my first step was to move to a significantly smaller apartment close to the hospital where I would receive cancer treatment, if necessary. Coincidentally, the hospital across the street from my new Seattle residence was called Swedish Hospital—fitting for a story centered around Swedish Death Cleaning. During the downsizing process, I meticulously organized my belongings. After digitizing precious mementos of my past, I generously donated them to local charities as I suspected my family would eventually discard them anyway.

My new micro-apartment was only 248 square feet, demanding mindful consideration of what I brought in—strictly limiting my things to the essentials of daily life. No longer could I thoughtlessly transfer boxes from one residence to the next, oblivious to their worth or impact on my life. The constrained square footage forced me to let go of my materialistic lifestyle. When I went shopping or browsed arts and crafts at Pike Place Market, the practical question, "Where am I going to put this?" forced me to leave behind any new treasures I considered buying. Nonetheless, the compensation for this modest space was an awe-inspiring view of the Seattle skyline framed by the backdrop of Puget Sound—an incredible and uncluttered space to write.

Then I faced my parking dilemma. My new building lacked parking facilities, forcing me to take a long walk downtown to mull over this predicament. Standing on an overpass above the bustling I-5 freeway in downtown Seattle, adjacent to the convention center, I observed an endless stream of cars and trucks sluggishly traversing through the city's core. This sight prompted me to reflect upon the countless hours and dollars wasted, not to mention the pollution caused by this inefficient movement of people.

Like most modern humans, I wholeheartedly embraced the belief that owning a car is essential. However, I began to consider the burdens that come with car ownership. In addition to the financial commitments, car ownership requires significant time and energy to maintain, clean, refuel, insure, repair, and worry about theft and damage. Moreover, I often felt pressured to replace my car whenever someone in my life acquired a shinier, sleeker, or sexier model.

This led me to contemplate the amount of energy and time that could be saved by not having a car. On the overpass, I made the decision to sell my car—a choice I have not regretted since. Living in an area with a near-perfect walkability rating with reliable public transportation was crucial for my car-free lifestyle. On the few occasions I needed a car, I utilized ride-sharing services like Uber or Lyft or rented a car from nearby Sea-Tac airport.

Now without a car, I had to be mindful of my actions. I decided to rent a U-Haul truck to transport the limited furniture that could fit into my new micro-apartment. Back at my previous residence, I digitized my valuable photos, vital documents, and mementos. Then, I decided to donate, discard, or recycle most of the remaining items. In my micro-apartment, I set up a small antique curio shelf where I showcased the few items that held the most significance to me and still evoked joyful memories— mostly artwork I had purchased on trips to Mexico.

In addition to decluttering my physical space, I needed to declutter my emotional and spiritual life as well. My wake-up call revealed to me that I had yet to truly uncover my authentic self and the purpose of my existence. Alongside heeding my doctor's advice and organizing my life affairs, I embarked on a profound journey of self-reflection, confronting the deeper questions of life.

Interestingly, the more I uncluttered my physical space, the clearer the answers to these deep life questions became. A profound realization washed over me as I paused to reflect on my life and confront my mortality. It became unmistakably clear that a profound link existed between an uncluttered life and an uncluttered soul. My brush with death revealed to me that material possessions were impeding my ability to embrace the fullness of life.

I began to imagine waking up every morning feeling light and free, unburdened by the weight of physical and emotional clutter accumulated over the years. I tried to picture a life filled with meaningful experiences, deep connections, and a sense of purpose that resonated with every fiber of my being. I began to realize this is not a far-fetched dream but a tangible reality that awaits anyone who embraces the transformative wisdom of Swedish Death Cleaning.

I began to realize the true essence of life is not tied to the accumulation and preservation of material possessions. Even cavemen and women were hunter-gatherers 2.5 million years ago. Shouldn't we, as modern beings, have evolved in understanding our purpose and meaning? Doesn't life offer far more than accumulating possessions that time inevitably erodes and thieves can snatch away? Perhaps Jesus alluded to our tendency to find identity in our possessions when he said, "For where your treasure is, there your heart will be also." (Matthew 6:19, NKJV).

About halfway through the Death Cleaning steps, I realized the wisdom of Swedish Death Cleaning is not about getting ready to die—it's about learning how to live! Why wait to live a richer and more fulfilling life?

The mindful principles of Swedish Death Cleaning encourage us to break free from the grip of consumerism and redefine our priorities. It challenges the notion that a meaningful life is measured by the number of possessions you accumulate. Instead, it invites us to focus on the quality of our experiences and relationships. It calls us to "measure your life in love," as Jonathan Larson famously wrote. By intentionally reducing the number of material possessions we own and releasing their hold on us, we create space for what truly brings us joy, meaning, purpose, and fulfillment.

Making a deliberate lifestyle change to curate our living spaces can enhance well-being and help us live in harmony with our true selves. We can learn to avoid emotional attachment to possessions and refrain from finding our identity in our things. Embracing this transformation demands patience, introspection, and self-compassion.

Swedish Death Cleaning challenges us to face our mortality and reflect on the legacy we wish to leave for our loved ones. Rather than presuming to know what is best for our heirs, we have honest conversations about our end-of-life arrangements. By being prepared, caring, and considerate, we establish a legacy that grants our loved ones the freedom and time to grieve and honor our lives, relieving them of the burden of sorting through and disposing of unwanted possessions after we're gone.

Now, let's begin exploring the practical steps necessary to

transform your life and physical space using the mindful wisdom of Swedish Death Cleaning. This life-changing adventure of discovering the essence of who you truly are will empower you to declutter your physical space while opening your heart, mind, and spirit.

Step 1. The Art of Swedish Death Cleaning: Keep, Donate, Sell, Recycle, or Trash

There's no better way to declutter your life and get your house in order than to take advantage of the principles of Swedish Death Cleaning. While getting your life in order, you begin to uncover who you are and find your meaning and purpose.

You accumulate belongings throughout your life, from sentimental items to forgotten trinkets, sometimes to the point of excess. This accumulation can become burdensome and overwhelming as the years go by, making it difficult to find what truly matters amidst the sea of stuff. Swedish Death Cleaning offers a practical and mindful approach to decluttering and organizing, providing a path to simplicity and clarity.

Finding purpose and meaning in life begins with an uncluttered lifestyle conducive to serenity and contemplation. The core of the Swedish Death Cleaning process revolves around sorting through and organizing your stuff. This step aims to make your living space life-inspiring and not possession-focused. Once sorted, you have five key options: keeping, giving, donating, selling, recycling, or trashing. Each option offers a unique approach to managing your possessions, allowing you to make conscious choices that align with your current life priorities. By exploring these options, you can create a clear roadmap to decluttering your life and leaving a positive legacy for your loved ones.

Your possessions can hold you back, tying you to the past or burdening you with unnecessary responsibilities. By consciously deciding what to keep and what to let go, you free yourself from the weight of excess and create space for new experiences and opportunities, allowing you to appreciate the present moment and cherish what truly matters in life. This act of letting go grants you a fresh perspective and a renewed sense of purpose, empowering you to curate your life according to your values and priorities.

As you delve into the various options for handling your possessions, you must remember there is no right or wrong choice. The key is approaching each decision with thoughtfulness, compassion, and a deep understanding of what truly matters to you. By engaging in Swedish Death Cleaning, you honor your life and the legacy you wish to leave behind.

I. Keep

In Swedish Death Cleaning, the term "keep" is "bevara," which encompasses the idea of preserving and holding onto items that hold personal significance. It urges us to assess the genuine value and significance of objects in our lives and make deliberate decisions about what to retain or pass on to future generations. Wherever you are on your life's journey, the profound principles of Swedish Death Cleaning have an equally transformative impact.

While it may be tempting to hold onto everything we own, Swedish Death Cleaning urges us to be discerning and create a clutter-free environment that is not burdened by excessive possessions, which prevents loved ones from dealing with a cluttered and disorganized estate after our passing. When evaluating the value and meaning of our possessions, it's important to remember that value is subjective and varies from person to person. The following tips can guide decision-making:

Assess Sentimental Value

Does this item bring you joy? Evaluate whether an object brings back cherished memories or represents a significant relationship. If it holds emotional significance, it may be worth keeping. Sentimental value is crucial in determining which items to keep during the Swedish Death Cleaning process. Objects that evoke strong emotions or hold cherished memories will likely be worth preserving. It could be a handwritten letter from a loved one, a memento from a vacation, or a photo album documenting precious moments. These items connect us to our past and provide a sense of continuity and comfort. When evaluating an item's sentimental value, consider the emotions it elicits and the memories it represents. If it brings you joy and holds deep personal meaning, it's worth putting in the "keep" pile.

Consider Practicality & Usefulness

Determine if an item serves a practical purpose in your current life or aligns with your needs. Let go of things that are outdated, redundant, or no longer relevant. While sentimentality is essential, assessing an item's practicality and usefulness is equally crucial. Keeping items that align with your present needs and lifestyle ensures that your living space remains organized and free from unnecessary clutter.

Reflect on Future Relevance

Contemplate whether an item will retain its value and relevance for future generations. Some possessions, such as family heirlooms, may be worth passing on as part of your legacy. Swedish Death Cleaning encourages you to think about the long-term relevance of your possessions.

Antique furniture or valuable collectibles are examples of possessions that might be worth preserving and passing on as part of your legacy. Reflect on whether these items have the potential to become cherished artifacts or if they have a broader historical or sentimental value that extends beyond your personal attachment to them. You can make informed decisions about which items to keep by considering their future relevance.

Prioritize Quality Over Quantity

Focus on keeping a few cherished possessions that bring genuine joy and serve a purpose rather than accumulating excessive clutter. In the spirit of Swedish Death Cleaning, it's essential to prioritize quality over quantity when it comes to the items we choose to keep. Rather than holding onto an abundance of possessions that provide little value or joy, focus on a select few that truly bring you happiness and serve a purpose.

The Swedish Death Cleaning philosophy aligns with the minimalist approach, emphasizing that a clutter-free living environment allows for greater clarity and appreciation of the things that matter most. By curating your possessions and keeping only those that bring you genuine joy, you can create a functional and meaningful space that can facilitate the awakening of a rich life. If all you can see in your room are things you need to dust, then it's time to prioritize quality over quantity.

Once you have determined which items to keep, it's essential to organize and store them in a way that promotes a clutter-free environment. Consider the following strategies:

Categorize & Label

Group similar items together and label containers, shelves, or drawers accordingly. This provides a clear overview and makes it easier to find specific items when needed. Categorize similar items and allocate designated spaces for each category. For example, you can group books together, store kitchen utensils in the same drawer, or organize clothing by type. Use labels, tags, or Post-it Notes to identify categories or the contents of containers, shelves, or drawers. This practice not only ensures that your items are easily accessible but also helps you maintain an organized living space.

Create Designated Spaces

Establish specific areas or storage solutions for different categories of items, such as sentimental objects, critical documents, and valuable belongings. This helps maintain order and prevents things from becoming scattered. Designate specific areas in your living space for different categories of items. For instance, create a space for sentimental objects, where you can display items that hold emotional value.

Allocate a separate area for essential documents, such as passports, insurance papers, or legal documents, ensuring they are easily accessible, well-protected, and all in one place. Additionally, have a dedicated space for valuable belongings like tools, cleaning supplies, or everyday essentials. By assigning specific spaces for different categories of items, you prevent them from getting mixed up and ensure that everything has its designated place.

Living in my micro-apartment has taught me that even the slightest hint of clutter can disrupt the overall appearance of the space. Therefore, I have developed a meticulous habit of promptly putting away every item in its designated spot. By adhering to this practice, I ensure that my living environment remains pristine and unencumbered, allowing me to bask in the serenity that comes with a clutter-free home.

The benefits of this organized lifestyle extend beyond mere aesthetics. With everything in its rightful place, I can effortlessly locate any item I need, saving precious time and eliminating unnecessary stress. Furthermore, by consistently practicing tidiness, I have cultivated a sense of discipline and orderliness that permeates other aspects of my life.

Maximize Vertical & Hidden Storage

Utilize vertical space by installing shelves or hanging storage units to make the most of the available room without cluttering surfaces. Additionally, consider hidden storage solutions like under-bed storage boxes or ottomans with hidden compartments to keep items out of sight. In small or compact living spaces, maximizing storage efficiency becomes crucial.

Regularly Reassess & Declutter

Periodically reassess the items you choose to keep and consider whether they continue to hold value and meaning in your life. Regular decluttering sessions help maintain a clutter-free environment and prevent unnecessary accumulation. Swedish Death Cleaning is an ongoing process that requires periodic reassessment and decluttering. As time passes, our needs, tastes, and priorities may change. Therefore, it's essential to regularly revisit the items you have chosen to keep and evaluate whether they continue to hold value and meaning in your life. By conducting regular decluttering sessions, you can ensure that your living environment remains organized, relevant, and free from unnecessary accumulation.

By carefully considering which items to keep, evaluating their value and meaning, and employing effective organizational strategies, you can create a living environment that reflects your true priorities. Swedish Death Cleaning encourages you to let go of unnecessary possessions and focus on preserving what truly matters, leading to a more intentional and clutter-free life.

II. Donate

In the Swedish Death Cleaning method, the concept of "donate" holds significant importance. It encourages individuals to let go of their possessions and gives them a new purpose by contributing to those in need or donating to charitable organizations. The Swedish word for "donate" is "donera," embodying the spirit of generosity and compassion underlying this practice.

Benefits of Donating

Donating items as part of the Swedish Death Cleaning process can have numerous benefits, both for the giver and the recipients. Here are some key advantages:

Helping Others

Donating allows you to make a positive impact on the lives of others. By giving away items you no longer need, you assist those who may not have the means to afford them. Your act of kindness can bring joy, comfort, and practical support to individuals or families facing challenging circumstances. Whether donating clothing to someone who lacks proper attire or providing household essentials to a family starting anew, your donations can make a meaningful difference in someone's life.

Decluttering with Purpose

Donating serves a dual purpose by helping you declutter your living space while knowing that your belongings will benefit someone else. This process allows you to create a more organized and peaceful environment, free from unnecessary possessions that may hold you back emotionally or physically. When you let go of items that no longer serve you, you make room for new experiences. Decluttering with purpose can be cathartic and liberating, allowing you to focus on what truly matters.

Environmental Responsibility

Donating items instead of discarding them helps reduce waste and promotes environmental sustainability. By giving your possessions a second life, you contribute to the circular economy and reduce the demand for new resources. This eco-conscious approach aligns with the Swedish Death Cleaning philosophy of mindful and responsible living. It's an opportunity to embrace sustainability by minimizing your ecological footprint and making choices that benefit the planet.

Potential Donation Recipients

There are several options to consider when it comes to finding suitable donation recipients. Here are some common choices:

Local Shelters

Homeless shelters, women's shelters, and organizations that support individuals in crisis often appreciate donations. These establishments typically welcome clothing, bedding, personal care items, and household essentials. Contact local shelters to inquire about their specific needs and guidelines for accepting donations. They can provide valuable information on how to contribute effectively to their programs and assist those in need within your community.

Thrift Stores

Thrift stores, charity shops, or second-hand stores are popular destinations for donated items. These organizations resell donated goods at affordable prices, generating funds to support various community programs. Furniture, clothing, kitchenware, books, and toys are commonly accepted items. Research local thrift stores to learn about their acceptance policies and preferred donation hours.

Community Organizations

Many community organizations, such as schools, libraries, or community centers, often welcome donations to enhance their services and programs. Books, educational materials, sports equipment, and art supplies are examples of items that can find new homes and benefit the local community. Reach out to these organizations to understand their specific needs and how your donations can contribute to their initiatives. By supporting community organizations, you foster a sense of belonging within your community.

Nonprofit Organizations

Research nonprofit organizations in your area that align with the causes you support. These organizations often have specific needs for donations, such as medical equipment or specialized items for individuals with disabilities. Reach out to them to understand their requirements and arrange for donations. By targeting your contributions to specific causes, you can ensure that your items have a direct and meaningful impact on the communities or individuals you care about.

Sorting and Transporting Items for Donation

Efficiently sorting and transporting items for donation can streamline the Swedish Death Cleaning process. Here are some practical suggestions to help you in this endeavor:

Categorize and Label

Begin by categorizing items into broad groups, such as clothing, household items, books, and electronics. Label boxes or bags accordingly to ensure easy identification. This process simplifies the sorting and donation process and helps you keep track of what you plan to donate. By organizing your items into logical categories, you can streamline the entire process, making it easier to identify and prepare donations.

Check Donation Guidelines

Different donation recipients may have specific guidelines regarding the condition and types of items they accept.

Before donating, familiarize yourself with their requirements. For example, some organizations may only take lightly used clothing, while others may have restrictions on electronics or large furniture. By understanding these guidelines, you can ensure that your donations are appropriate and useful for the recipients.

Clean and Repair

Ensure that the items you plan to give away are clean and in good condition before donating. Wash clothing, wipe down surfaces, and repair any minor damages whenever possible. This consideration shows respect for the recipients and helps maintain the quality of donated items. Taking the time to clean and repair your donations demonstrates your thoughtfulness and ensures that the recipients receive items they can immediately use and enjoy.

Transportation Logistics

If you have many items to donate or heavy furniture, consider renting a van or truck for transportation. Coordinate with the donation recipient to determine the best time for drop-off or inquire if they offer pick-up services. Proper planning ensures a smooth and efficient donation process. By arranging transportation logistics in advance, you can avoid unnecessary stress and ensure that your donations reach their intended destinations effectively.

Donating items as part of the Swedish Death Cleaning method allows you to extend the life of your possessions and bring joy to others.

III. Sell

In the Swedish Death Cleaning method, selling items holds great significance. It not only allows you to declutter your living space but also provides an opportunity to earn some extra money or fund future experiences. The process of selling involves carefully assessing the value of your belongings and selecting the right selling platforms to reach potential buyers. In this section, we will explore the concept of selling in Swedish Death Cleaning, discuss strategies for determining item value, and provide tips on organizing, pricing, and advertising items effectively.

In Swedish Death Cleaning, selling, or "sälja," involves parting ways with items through a transactional process. This mindset helps you detach emotionally from your possessions and recognize their value to others. By embracing the act of selling, you transfer belongings and ensure they find a new purpose in someone else's life.

Selling during the Swedish Death Cleaning process can be empowering. It helps create a more organized living space while generating extra income for future endeavors or causes close to your heart. Knowing what your items are worth is essential to making informed decisions about what to keep and what to discard.

Here are some strategies to assess item worth:

Research

Conduct thorough research to understand the current market value of similar items. Online platforms, antique stores, and appraisal services offer valuable insights. Look for recent sales of comparable items to get an idea of what buyers are willing to pay.

Condition

Consider the condition of each item. Well-maintained and functional possessions generally hold more value than worn, damaged, or outdated ones. Be honest about the condition and adjust your expectations accordingly. Take note of any repairs or restorations that have been done and factor those into the value as well.

Rarity and Demand

Assess the rarity and demand for your items. Unique, limited edition or highly sought-after objects tend to command higher prices. Research whether there are collectors or enthusiasts specifically interested in the type of items you have. Consider reaching out to niche communities or forums to gauge interest and potential buyers.

Selecting the right selling platforms is crucial to maximize your chances of finding buyers. Consider these popular options:

Online Marketplaces

Websites like eBay, Craigslist, and Facebook Marketplace, and specialized platforms such as Etsy provide a vast reach and connect you with potential buyers worldwide. Take advantage of the large audience these platforms offer, but also be prepared for shipping logistics and associated costs.

Consignment Stores

These stores handle pricing, advertising, and customer interactions on your behalf. They can be a convenient option if you prefer a hands-off approach. Research local consignment stores and understand their terms and commission fees before deciding.

Yard Sales or Flea Markets

Hosting a yard sale or participating in local flea markets allows you to engage with buyers in person and sell multiple items at once. This option can be particularly beneficial for items that may not have significant resale value but can still find interested buyers at lower price points. Ensure you adhere to any local regulations or permits required for hosting such events.

Follow these tips to sell your belongings successfully:

Organization

Sort your items into categories and create a dedicated space to store them until sold. This facilitates locating and showcasing items to potential buyers. Keep track of what items are listed on which platforms to avoid confusion and ensure efficient management.

Pricing

Set reasonable and competitive prices based on market research, considering item condition, brand, and rarity. Be prepared to negotiate but also know your bottom line. If you're uncertain about the value of an item, you can consider getting a professional appraisal to ensure you're pricing it appropriately.

Item Descriptions

Write detailed and accurate descriptions, highlighting key features, conditions, and relevant history. Including clear, well-lit photographs enhances the appeal of your listings. Be transparent about any flaws or imperfections and provide measurements or specifications when necessary. A comprehensive and honest description helps build trust with potential buyers.

Advertising

Maximize visibility by utilizing platform features. Share listings on social media, relevant groups or forums, and consider paid advertising options. Engage with potential buyers promptly and courteously to build trust and encourage inquiries. Respond to questions or comments in a timely manner and be prepared to provide additional information or photographs if requested.

Organizing, pricing, and advertising effectively increases the likelihood of finding interested buyers and achieving successful sales. Throughout the process, be patient and prepared for the emotional aspect of parting ways with your belongings. Remember that one of the goals of Swedish Death Cleaning is to declutter and ensure that your items find new purpose and bring joy to others.

IV. Recycle

In Swedish Death Cleaning, where we declutter and organize our belongings, one crucial aspect is finding responsible and environmentally friendly disposal methods for items that cannot be reused or donated. While the goal is to minimize waste and reduce our ecological footprint, recycling plays a vital role in ensuring that materials are repurposed and reintroduced into the manufacturing cycle. The Swedish term "Återvinning" signifies the act of giving items a second life by transforming them into new products, reducing the need for virgin materials and minimizing environmental impact.

Environmentally Friendly Disposal Methods

When engaging in Swedish Death Cleaning, we aim to approach the process with mindfulness and consideration for the planet. Choosing environmentally friendly disposal methods for items we cannot reuse or donate is an essential part of this practice. By recycling these materials, we divert them from landfills, conserve resources, and minimize energy consumption and greenhouse gas emissions associated with extracting and manufacturing new materials.

Identifying Recyclable Materials

While the specifics of recycling programs may vary based

on location, it is essential to understand what materials are recyclable. Common recyclable materials include paper, cardboard, glass, aluminum and steel cans, plastic bottles and containers, and certain types of electronics. However, it's important to note that the recyclability of certain materials may depend on the local recycling infrastructure, which can differ from region to region. Contact your municipal waste management department for specific information on what materials can be recycled in your area.

Locating Appropriate Recycling Locations

Once you have identified recyclable materials, the next step is to find suitable recycling facilities or programs. Start by researching recycling centers or drop-off locations in your community. Many municipalities provide recycling collection services, while others may have dedicated recycling centers where you can drop off materials.

Online resources and recycling directories can also assist in locating specialized recycling programs for specific items, such as electronics, batteries, or hazardous waste. These programs ensure that these items are handled properly and do not pose a risk to the environment or human health.

Reducing Your Ecological Footprint

Swedish Death Cleaning encourages individuals to embrace sustainable practices, and responsible recycling is an integral part of this mindset. By incorporating recycling into our decluttering process, we actively contribute to a more environmentally conscious lifestyle. Beyond recycling, there are other actions we can take to reduce our ecological footprint further. Consider minimizing waste by adopting the principles of reduction and reuse. Before disposing of an item, explore alternative uses or creative ways to repurpose it. By extending the lifespan of objects, we can reduce the demand for new products and conserve resources.

Furthermore, by engaging in mindful consumption and refraining from excessive purchases, we can effectively curb clutter buildup and minimize waste from the outset. Making conscientious choices about the items we incorporate into our lives paves the way for a more sustainable future. Recycling plays an integral part in the Swedish Death Cleaning method, as it grants materials a second chance and lessens our environmental impact. By comprehending the principles of recycling, recognizing recyclable materials, and locating suitable recycling facilities or programs, we can embrace responsible and sustainable practices, actively contribute to the circular economy, reduce our ecological footprint, and foster a cleaner and more sustainable world for future generations.

V. Trash

In Swedish Death Cleaning, the term for "trash" is "Skräp." This word embodies the essence of items that have become useless, obsolete or hold no value. Skräp represents the physical clutter that can accumulate over a lifetime and, if not addressed, can burden both the living and those who may be left behind. Understanding this term helps us recognize the significance of letting go of possessions that have lost their purpose.

Letting Go of Items with No Value or Purpose

One of the core principles of Swedish Death Cleaning is acknowledging the necessity of letting go. In the Trash stage, it is essential to embrace the idea that some possessions no longer hold any value or purpose in our lives. These items may include broken or damaged objects, outdated electronics, worn-out clothing, or expired household products. While it can be challenging to part with belongings we once cherished, it is important to remember that our attachment to these items does not define our memories or the experiences we hold dear.

By removing items with no value or purpose from our physical surroundings, we create space for new opportunities and experiences. The process of decluttering allows us to reevaluate what truly matters to us and encourages us to focus on the things that bring us joy and fulfillment. Letting go of possessions that serve no purpose frees us from the burden of excess and paves the way for a more intentional and meaningful life.

Disposing of Items Properly

Once we have identified items as trash or skräp, it is crucial to dispose of them responsibly. Engaging in environmentally friendly practices during the disposal process aligns with the values of Swedish Death Cleaning. Whether we take our unwanted items to the dump, place them in our garbage cans, or recycle them, we want to make sure we dispose of things we no longer need in an environmentally responsible manner.

The Cathartic Effect of Releasing Physical Clutter

Swedish Death Cleaning recognizes that decluttering and letting go of possessions can have a profound impact on our mental well-being. By acknowledging the importance of releasing physical clutter, we open the door to emotional and psychological freedom. Here's how the Trash stage of Swedish Death Cleaning can have a cathartic effect:

Clearing Mental Space

Physical clutter often translates into mental clutter. The act of letting go of unnecessary items allows us to clear our minds and create space for new ideas, thoughts, and experiences. It provides an opportunity to focus on what truly matters, leading to increased clarity and mental well-being.

Letting Go of Emotional Baggage

Belongings can be tied to memories, emotions, or even unfinished chapters in our lives. When we let go of items that no longer serve us, we release the emotional weight associated with them. This process can be liberating, allowing us to move forward with a lighter spirit and a renewed sense of emotional well-being.

Embracing Change and Growth

Swedish Death Cleaning is not just about decluttering our physical spaces but also about embracing change and personal growth. By letting go of possessions, we become more adaptable and open to new experiences. We learn to detach our identity from material possessions and focus on the intangible aspects of life that bring us joy and fulfillment.

Celebrate each step of the decluttering process, including disposing of items that no longer serve a purpose. Recognize the impact of your actions, not just on your immediate surroundings but also on the environment and your own well-being. By actively participating in the Trash stage, you contribute to a more sustainable future and create a sense of harmony within yourself. Our relationship with our possessions is complex, and it evolves over time. Embrace the fluidity of this process and allow yourself to adapt and grow along the way.

Step 1 Conclusion

Throughout this step, we have emphasized the joy and liberation experienced through the process of Swedish Death Cleaning. By intentionally curating our possessions and letting go of excess, we create physical and mental space that allows us to focus on what truly matters in our lives. The act of decluttering becomes an opportunity for self-reflection and self-discovery, enabling us to align our surroundings with our values and aspirations. In the next step, we will discuss sharing our legacy with family members and loved ones. By passing down cherished possessions, we not only establish a meaningful connection with our family history but also ensure that these items continue to be treasured and appreciated. Sharing stories and memories associated with these possessions can strengthen family bonds and preserve our legacy for future generations.

Step 2. Share Your Legacy
with Loved Ones

G iving away possessions to family members or loved ones is a significant facet of the Swedish Death Cleaning process. It surpasses mere decluttering; it represents an opportunity to bestow your legacy upon others and ensure that cherished items find appreciative new homes. This section delves into the significance of giving to family and friends, explores the diverse perspectives individuals may hold concerning these objects, and offers guidance on documenting family heritage stories.

The act of giving possessions to family members holds a deep significance in many cultures. In Swedish Death Cleaning, this act is particularly cherished as it allows for the continuation of family traditions and the preservation of memories. By passing down cherished items, you are not only transferring physical belongings but also the emotions and stories attached to them. These objects carry with them the essence of your experiences, values, and personal history, making them valuable heirlooms that connect generations.

When considering the act of giving to family, it's important to recognize that different individuals may have varying perspectives on the value of objects. While some possessions may hold great sentimental significance for you, others may not hold the same emotional weight for your loved ones. It's crucial to engage in open and honest conversations about the items you wish to pass down. This dialogue will help you understand the desires and preferences of your family members, allowing you to make informed decisions about what to give and to whom.

As you go through the process of giving possessions to family members, it is essential to approach them with care and sensitivity. While it is natural to have attachments to certain items, it's important to remember that the act of giving is about sharing your legacy and passing on meaningful objects to those who will appreciate them. Be open to the perspectives and desires of your loved ones and consider their interests and preferences when making decisions about what to give.

Giving away possessions to family members is a significant step in the Swedish Death Cleaning process. The generous and thoughtful step allows you to share your legacy, preserve family traditions, and strengthen familial bonds.

I. The Joy of Passing Down Cherished Possessions

One of the most rewarding aspects of decluttering and Swedish Death Cleaning is the opportunity it provides to pass down cherished possessions to our loved ones. The act of giving these items to family members not only declutters our own lives but also allows us to witness the delight and appreciation on their faces as they receive these heirlooms. In this way, we actively contribute to the continuation of family traditions and the preservation of familial connections, fostering a sense of shared heritage and identity.

Each possession we pass down carries with it a unique story—a tale of its own and a place in our family's history. It could be a piece of jewelry that has been passed down from one generation to another, a treasured book collection that has provided knowledge, inspiration, and solace, or a family recipe that has been carefully preserved and shared throughout the years.

When we give these cherished possessions to our loved ones, we offer them more than just material objects. We offer them a piece of our own journey, a glimpse into our experiences, values, and beliefs. Through these possessions, we share our personal histories and the lessons we have learned along the way. Our loved ones can hold in their hands the same jewelry worn by their great-grandparents or read the very books that once captivated their ancestors. In this exchange, we create a bridge between generations, allowing the past to live on in the present and the future.

Passing down cherished possessions is an opportunity to nurture and strengthen family bonds. It opens up avenues for conversation and storytelling, as each item has its own tale to tell. When we give away these possessions, we invite our loved ones to engage with their family history, encouraging them to ask questions, share their own memories, and connect with their roots. These interactions foster a deeper understanding of our collective past and help forge a sense of belonging and continuity within the family unit.

In addition to the emotional and sentimental significance, passing down cherished possessions can also provide practical benefits. These items often hold financial value, and by giving them to our loved ones, we provide them with tangible assets that can support their future endeavors. Whether it's a valuable antique, a piece of artwork, or a collection of rare books, these possessions can serve as a form of inheritance, offering financial security and opportunities for personal growth.

The joy of passing down cherished possessions is a central aspect of Swedish Death Cleaning and decluttering. By giving these items to our loved ones, we not only declutter our own lives but also contribute to the continuation of family traditions, the preservation of familial connections, and the fostering of a shared heritage and identity.

II. Communicate Your Intentions with Heirs

In the process of Swedish Death Cleaning, when you reach the stage of giving away your possessions to loved ones, it is important to approach this task with empathy and understanding. What holds significance for you may not hold the same meaning for someone else. Their idea of value might differ, and they may have limited space or specific requirements that influence their choices.

It is essential to approach the process of giving away cherished possessions with careful consideration and open communication. While some items may hold deep sentimental value to us, they may not have the same meaning for our loved ones. It's crucial to have honest conversations with family members, understand their interests and desires, and ensure that the items we give are truly valued and appreciated. This collaborative approach not only strengthens family connections but also ensures that our possessions find new homes where they will be treasured for generations to come.

When deciding which items to give to family members, it is helpful to engage in open and respectful conversations. This will help you gain insight into their interests, needs, and willingness to accept certain things. By understanding their perspectives, you can make more informed decisions and ensure that your gifts are genuinely appreciated.

Begin by initiating a dialogue with your family members about their preferences and desires. Ask them if there are specific items they would like to inherit or if there are any sentimental objects they associate with fond memories. Such conversations can provide valuable guidance in determining which possessions would hold the most meaning for them.

Keep in mind that the goal is to pass on items that will genuinely be appreciated and cherished by the recipients rather than burdening them with unwanted or burdensome possessions. By respecting their choices and involving them in the decision-making process, you are more likely to give away items that align with their values and enhance their lives. It is also crucial to consider the practical aspects of passing down possessions. Some objects may require significant maintenance or storage space, which may not be feasible for some recipients.

II. Share Heritage Stories About the Significance of Family Heirlooms

Family heirlooms hold a special place in our hearts and homes. They are tangible connections to our past, carrying within them stories of our ancestors and the traditions that have shaped our family's history. Swedish Death Cleaning presents an opportunity to not only lighten the load but also to share the rich heritage stories associated with these cherished possessions. In this section, we explore the importance of sharing heritage stories about the significance of family heirlooms and how they can strengthen the bond between loved ones.

Preservation of Family History

Family heirlooms are vessels of history, carrying the memories, experiences, and values of those who came before us. By sharing stories about these objects, we pass down the narratives that define our family's identity. For example, a silver pocket watch handed down from one generation to the next may hold stories of determination, hard work, or a significant event in the family's history. By discussing these stories, we ensure that future generations understand and appreciate their roots.

Strengthening Family Connections

Sharing heritage stories about family heirlooms creates opportunities for meaningful conversations and shared experiences. It allows family members to come together and learn about their collective past, fostering a sense of belonging and unity. When the significance of an heirloom is explained, it becomes more than just an object—it becomes a symbol of the shared values and traditions that tie the family together.

Passing Down Values & Life Lessons

Family heirlooms often come with accompanying stories that reflect the values and life lessons of our ancestors. For instance, a handwritten recipe book passed down through generations may hold recipes that were cherished for their simplicity and nourishment, teaching us the value of tradition, craftsmanship, and the importance of gathering around the table. By sharing these stories, we impart wisdom and lessons learned from the experiences of our forebears.

Inspiring Future Generations

When we share heritage stories about family heirlooms, we inspire curiosity and a sense of pride in younger generations. These stories ignite their imagination, encouraging them to explore their roots and understand their place in the family narrative. By fostering a connection to the past, we inspire a sense of responsibility to carry forward the family's traditions and values.

Family heirlooms are more than just physical objects; they are gateways to our shared history. By sharing heritage stories about the significance of these cherished possessions, we preserve our family's legacy, strengthen family connections, pass down values and life lessons, honor our ancestors' contributions, and inspire future generations.

Step 2 Conclusion

In this step, we highlighted the importance of sharing our legacy with loved ones. Whether it be a family heirloom, or an important family story, sharing our legacy is an important step in the Swedish Death Cleaning process. By taking the time to share these narratives and memories, you can ensure that your loved ones have a deeper appreciation for the items they receive and a stronger connection to their family's past. In the next step, we will explore the importance of digital preservation, focusing specifically on preserving cherished photographs, vital documents, and sentimental memorabilia that we may no longer desire to retain physically but wish to safeguard their cherished memories.

Step 3. Digitize Old Photos, Documents & Memorabilia

I n the process of Swedish Death Cleaning, the preservation of memories takes center stage as an essential step toward achieving a clutter-free life. By embracing the practice of digitizing vital documents and capturing photos of cherished memorabilia, you can ensure that the essence of these items is preserved, even if they choose to let go of them physically.

Living in the digital age, where technology permeates nearly every aspect of our lives, it is only natural that we extend its benefits to the preservation of our most treasured memories. Digitizing photographs, vital documents, and memorabilia not only aids in decluttering our physical spaces but also offers a secure and convenient way to store, access, and share these important items. It enables us to safeguard our memories against the ravages of time, loss, or unforeseen circumstances, such as accidents or natural disasters. Furthermore, by embracing digital alternatives, we can significantly reduce paper clutter, contributing to a more sustainable and environmentally friendly lifestyle.

I. Digitize Old Photos

Preserving cherished memories is an essential part of the Swedish Death Cleaning process. As you embark on the journey of decluttering and simplifying your living space, it's crucial to find ways to safeguard the sentimental value attached to old photos, documents, and memorabilia. Fortunately, with the advancement of technology, digitizing these precious items has become more accessible than ever before.

One of the simplest and most convenient ways to digitize old photos is by utilizing the camera on your smartphone. Almost everyone carries a smartphone with a high-quality camera these days, making it an ideal tool for capturing images of your cherished photographs. Google also offers an app called PhotoScan which we will discuss at the end of this section.

Organize Your Old Photos

Begin by collecting and organizing the photos you wish to digitize. You can organize them by date, family group, importance, or whatever makes the most sense to you. This initial step helps you create a sense of purpose and prioritize the most significant photos.

Find a Well-Lit Area

Look for a well-lit spot in your home where you can lay out the photos. Natural light is preferable, as it helps capture the details and colors accurately. Avoid using flash, as it can create unwanted glare or reflections on the images.

Steady Your Phone

To capture clear and focused photos, stabilize your phone by placing it on a flat surface or using a tripod if available. This will help prevent blurriness caused by shaky hands. Alternatively, you can use a phone stand or a smartphone tripod adapter to secure your device and achieve consistent results.

Capture the Photos

Open the camera app on your smartphone and position it directly above the photo you want to digitize. Make sure the entire picture is within the frame and aligned as straight as possible. Tap the screen to focus, and if necessary, adjust the exposure to ensure the image is neither too bright nor too dark.

Experiment with different angles to find the one that captures the photo best.

Take Multiple Shots

It's always a good practice to capture multiple shots of each photo, slightly varying the angles and distances. This will increase the chances of obtaining a high-quality digital image. Don't rush this process; take your time to ensure each photo is captured in the best possible way.

Review & Edit

Once you have captured the photos, review them in your phone's gallery. Delete any duplicates or blurry shots, keeping only the best versions. Most smartphones offer basic editing tools, allowing you to enhance the brightness, contrast, or color balance if needed. However, it's advisable to preserve the original state of the photo as much as possible unless there are significant issues that require correction.

PhotoScan by Google

While using the camera on your phone is a convenient method for digitizing old photos, there is also a dedicated app called PhotoScan by Google that can simplify the process even further. This app is designed specifically for digitizing printed photos, eliminating glare, and providing tools to ensure high-quality scans. One of my relatives used PhotoScan to digitize and organize all of his family's important photos and highly recommends this app.

PhotoScan by Google provides a step-by-step guide to help you achieve excellent results: Download the app: Visit the official website of PhotoScan by Google (https://www.google.com/photos/scan) to learn more about the app and its features. From there, you can download the app through Google Play for Android devices or the App Store for iOS devices.

By using your smartphone's camera or the dedicated PhotoScan app, you can efficiently digitize your old photos and ensure they are safely preserved for years to come. This process not only declutters your physical space but also opens up new possibilities for sharing and reliving cherished memories in the digital realm. Consider posting some of these newly digitized old photos on Facebook to family and friends.

The goal is to capture the essence and emotional significance of your old photos, allowing you to revisit them whenever you want and pass them down to future generations. Once you have digitized your old photos, you can either give them away to family members or discard them. Old photos cannot be recycled and should be placed in the trash. When I digitized my old photos, I kept a handful of them as cherished mementos.

II. Digitize Important Documents

Preserving and digitizing important documents is an essential step in the process of Swedish Death Cleaning. By converting your physical documents into digital files, you not only declutter your living space but also ensure the long-term preservation and easy accessibility of these vital records. In this section, we will explore various techniques and strategies for digitizing important documents, as well as discuss different options for digital storage.

Gather the Necessary Equipment

The best way to digitize documents is with a digital scanner, but you can also use your smartphone to digitize vital paperwork. Each method has its advantages. A scanner can provide precise and high-resolution scans, ensuring optimal image quality, while a smartphone offers convenience and portability, allowing you to scan documents on the go. I personally digitized all of my vital documents with my smartphone.

Sort & Organize

Before scanning your documents, take the time to sort through them and identify those that hold significant value or require preservation. This step allows you to prioritize your efforts and focus on the most important documents. Start by categorizing your documents based on their nature or relevance, such as legal documents, personal letters, certificates, or any other categories that suit your needs.

Carefully examine each document and consider its significance. Some documents may have sentimental value, such as handwritten letters or cards, while others may be essential for legal or financial purposes, such as contracts or tax records. By organizing your documents into categories, you create a systematic approach to digitization, making the files easier to find later.

Set Up a Scanning Station

Creating a comfortable and well-lit scanning station is crucial for efficient digitization. Look for a space with ample lighting to ensure clear and legible scans. Natural light is preferable, but if that's not available, use a desk lamp or other light source to provide sufficient illumination. Additionally, ensure that you have enough space to handle your documents efficiently. A clutter-free environment will streamline the scanning process and minimize the risk of misplacing or damaging any papers.

Scan the Documents

If you're using a scanner, place each document individually on the scanner bed, making sure to align it properly to capture the entire page. Adjust the settings on your scanner to ensure optimal quality, including resolution and file format. Higher resolutions are preferable for preserving intricate details but keep in mind that larger files may require more storage space.

If you're using a smartphone, ensure that the camera is set to its highest quality setting. Hold the phone steady and capture the document in good lighting conditions. You may find it helpful to use a document scanning app that automatically detects the edges and enhances the image quality to enhance the scanning process.

Organize Digital Files

After scanning, organizing the scanned documents in a digital format is essential. Create folders on your computer or cloud storage service and name them according to the categories you established earlier. This step helps maintain a logical structure for your digital files and makes it easier to locate specific documents when needed.

Consider creating subfolders within each main category to further organize your documents. For example, if you have a legal documents folder, you can create subfolders property-related documents or estate planning documents. By organizing your files, you can quickly navigate through your digitized collection and find the document you need without any hassle.

Digital Document Storage

Once you have digitized your documents and organized them in a digital format, it is essential to implement backup strategies to prevent data loss. While digital files are generally more durable than physical documents, they can still be susceptible to accidental deletion, computer malfunctions, or data corruption. Therefore, it is crucial to back up your files regularly to ensure their long-term preservation.

Several reliable cloud storage options are available for storing your digitized photos and documents. Google Drive, Microsoft OneDrive, and Apple iCloud are popular choices that offer both free and paid plans with varying storage capacities. These services provide secure storage and convenient accessibility to your files from any device with an internet connection. Additionally, Amazon offers a free online photo storage service called Amazon Photos, which can be used for storing your digitized photos.

Apart from cloud storage, it is also advisable to create redundant backups of your important documents. This can be achieved by copying your digitized files to external hard drives, thumb drives/flash drives, or SSD external hard drives. These physical storage devices are readily available for purchase and offer an additional layer of security for your digital files. Storing your digitized documents on multiple cloud servers, as well as having a local backup on a thumb drive, ensures that your files are protected even in the event of a service outage or hardware failure.

Remember to keep your backup drives in a safe and secure location, preferably away from your primary storage devices. This reduces the risk of losing both your original documents and digital copies in case of theft, fire, or natural disasters.

Go Paperless on Bills & Statements

One of the easiest ways to reduce paper clutter is by switching to electronic billing and statements. Contact your utility providers, banks, credit card companies, and other relevant institutions to inquire about their paperless options. Many companies now offer email delivery or provide online portals where you can access your documents. By opting for electronic delivery, you not only save paper but also simplify the process of managing and organizing your bills and statements.

After digitizing your critical documents, it is essential to assess which ones can be shredded, which ones should be retained, and the duration of their retention. Legal and government documents often have specific retention requirements that should be followed diligently. Seeking advice from a specialist is recommended to ascertain the appropriate duration for preserving the original copies of these crucial documents.

III. Digitize Memorabilia

In addition to digitizing old photos and important documents, you can digitally capture physical objects, including memorabilia. This process enables you to preserve the essence of these items, minimizing physical clutter and creating a lasting legacy for future generations. Once these items are digitized, you can choose to let go of the physical objects by giving them away, recycling them, or disposing of them, while still retaining the digital memories of these cherished items.

Using your smartphone to take photographs of family heirlooms, such as paintings, furniture, or artwork, is a simple way to document your family's history digitally. Take high-quality photographs of each item, capturing their unique features, craftsmanship, and any distinguishing marks or signatures. Pay attention to the lighting, composition, and angles to ensure that the photographs accurately represent the physical attributes of the objects. Consider including close-up shots that highlight intricate details and textures, as well as wider shots that provide context and perspective.

Audio recordings can also be a powerful medium for capturing memories. Record yourself describing each object's significance, sharing associated stories, or even reading letters or documents accompanying the items. Audio recordings bring a sense of intimacy and can evoke powerful emotions when revisited in the future.

By combining the documentation of family heritage stories with digital records of the items themselves, you create a comprehensive archive that captures the essence of your family's legacy. This archive serves as a treasure trove of memories, ensuring that the significance of the items you give to family members endures through time. It becomes a valuable resource for future generations to learn about their roots, appreciate their heritage, and feel a sense of connection to their ancestors.

Keep in mind that this process is not just about preserving the objects themselves but also about capturing their stories, emotions, and memories. Documenting and digitizing these elements let you let go of the physical clutter while preserving the intangible aspects that truly matter. It is a profound way to honor your past, cherish the present, and create a lasting legacy for the future.

Let Go of Memorabilia Once Digitized

Once you have digitally captured your memorabilia, you are free to decide whether to keep them, pass them along to another family member, or dispose of them. The process of digitization liberates you from the burden of physical possessions and grants you the freedom to make deliberate choices about what to do with them.

Every family has unique stories and treasures that hold sentimental value. In my own family, we had a beautiful oak roll-top desk that had been passed down through generations. However, this classic piece of family history weighed over 350 pounds and was very fragile. As a family, we decided to digitally preserve and recycle the desk rather than burden future generations.

We captured the intricate carvings, the worn-out leather writing surface, and even the hidden compartments that had held secrets for years. Once we completed the digital documentation, we hired a handyman to dismantle the desk and take it to a recycling center. Having preserved the essence of this family heirloom, we could now pass along the memories associated with this heavy piece of furniture without having to worry about the space and care keeping it would require.

When you take the time to capture your belongings digitally, you are preserving their essence, memories, and sentimental value. By transforming physical items into digital files, you ensure their long-term preservation while reducing the physical space they occupy. This reduction in physical clutter can profoundly impact your overall well-being, providing you with a sense of calm and tranquility within your living environment.

Items that hold profound emotional significance or those you wish to pass down to future generations may be worth keeping in their physical form. These objects, such as heirlooms or personal mementos, can be treasured touchstones connecting you to your past and loved ones. Other objects may be valued in digital form, where the original is discarded. By digitizing items that may be too large to keep, you ensure their preservation for future generations while freeing up important physical space in the present.

Step 3 Conclusion

In this step, we explored the significance of preserving memories by digitizing old photos, critical documents, and family memorabilia. Swedish Death Cleaning helps us to declutter our physical spaces while creating a lasting legacy for future generations. By utilizing technology, we can convert our cherished mementos into digital formats, ensuring their longevity and easy access.

In the next step, we will discuss organizing our finances, creating a will, and sharing our funeral wishes with friends and loved ones. Taking the time to handle these tasks can relieve our loved ones of uncertainty and ensure our wishes are fulfilled.

Step 4. Leave an Uncluttered Legacy: Finances, Will, & Funeral Plans

We have explored the art of decluttering our physical possessions, simplifying our living spaces, and embracing a more intentional and meaningful life. Step 4 is a vital phase in the Swedish Death Cleaning process, where you get your finances in order, create a will, and let friends and loved ones know your funeral wishes. While this may initially seem like a departure from the physical act of tidying, it is integral to leaving an uncluttered legacy and ensuring a smooth transition for your loved ones once you are gone.

One of your primary motivations behind leaving an uncluttered legacy is to alleviate the stress and anxiety that often accompanies the aftermath of a loved one's passing. By proactively addressing financial matters, creating a will, and making funeral plans, you can ease the burden on your family members, allowing them to focus on the healing process rather than being overwhelmed by administrative tasks and decision-making.

Imagine the peace of mind that comes from knowing your family won't have to sort through piles of papers, scour endless bank statements, or agonize over funeral arrangements while grieving. By organizing your finances, establishing a clear will, and outlining your funeral preferences, you provide a sense of relief and clarity for your loved ones, allowing them the space to mourn and remember you without the additional stress of logistical challenges.

Furthermore, addressing these matters is not solely for the benefit of your family members—it is also an act of self-care and self-preservation. When you organize your finances, create a will, and make funeral plans, you gain peace of mind and clarity in your own life. You no longer carry the weight of uncertainty regarding your financial situation, nor do you leave your loved ones in a state of confusion about your wishes. By confronting these matters head-on, you actively shape the legacy you will leave behind, fostering a sense of empowerment and control over your own destiny.

Beyond personal belongings, it is crucial to consider the broader aspects of your financial legacy. While physical possessions hold sentimental value, your financial well-being and the structures you put in place have a lasting impact on the lives of those you leave behind. By taking the time to assess your financial situation, plan for potential contingencies, and provide for your loved ones, you create a foundation of stability and support for future generations. This holistic approach ensures that your legacy extends beyond the material realm, encompassing your values, wisdom, and the security of those you care about.

I. Organizing Your Finances

Money, in its essence, is a tool that allows us to navigate the world with a certain degree of freedom and security. We are often unsure of where our money goes or what our true financial standing is because we are entangled in an intricate web of financial complexity. By taking the time to assess our financial situation and streamline our accounts, we can gain clarity and peace of mind, ensuring that our loved ones are provided for when we are no longer here.

Gather Information on Assets, Debts, & Investments

Before you can make any meaningful progress in understanding your finances, it is essential to gather all pertinent information about your assets, debts, and investments. This includes taking stock of your bank accounts, investment portfolios, real estate holdings, and any outstanding loans or debts. By creating a comprehensive overview of your financial landscape, you can identify areas that require attention and make informed decisions about the future.

Start by organizing your financial documents in a central location. Gather bank statements, investment account statements, mortgage or rent documents, credit card statements, and any other relevant paperwork. This process may take some time, but it is an essential step in gaining a clear picture of your financial situation.

Once you have all the necessary documents, create a list of your assets, including bank accounts, investment accounts, real estate, and any valuable possessions. Make a note of any outstanding debts or loans you have, such as mortgages, car loans, or credit card balances. This comprehensive overview will serve as a foundation for understanding your financial health and making informed decisions.

Review & Update Beneficiaries

During our busy lives, it's easy to overlook the importance of reviewing and updating the beneficiaries on our financial accounts and life insurance policies. However, ensuring that the correct individuals are designated as beneficiaries is crucial to guarantee that your assets are distributed according to your wishes. Take the time to review your beneficiary designations and make any necessary changes, considering life events such as marriage, divorce, or childbirth.

Start by reviewing your bank accounts, retirement accounts, and life insurance policies. Contact the respective institutions or companies to update the beneficiaries as needed. Consider the implications of your choices and ensure that the designated beneficiaries align with your current intentions.

Keep a record of the updated beneficiary designations in a secure location and inform a trusted family member or executor of your estate about the changes you have made. This way, they will have the necessary information when the time comes to settle your affairs.

Seeking Professional Assistance for Estate Planning & Life

Insurance

While it's empowering to take control of your financial life, there are times when seeking professional assistance becomes necessary. Estate planning and life insurance are complex matters that require careful consideration and expertise. Engaging the services of a qualified estate planner or financial advisor can provide invaluable guidance in ensuring that you have enough funds to live on and that your family is taken care of once you are gone. They can help you navigate the intricacies of wills, trusts, and other legal instruments, tailoring them to your unique circumstances.

An estate planning attorney can assist you in creating a comprehensive estate plan. They will help you draft a will that reflects your wishes, establish trusts if necessary, and provide guidance on minimizing estate taxes and probate costs. An experienced attorney will ensure that your estate plan aligns with your goals and considers any specific concerns you may have.

Additionally, a financial advisor can help you evaluate your financial situation holistically and make recommendations for managing your assets effectively. They can provide guidance on investment strategies, retirement planning, and risk management. By working with a professional, you will be assured that your finances are in order and that your family is in good hands.

Communicate with Heirs about Your Finances & Beneficiaries

Open and honest communication with your loved ones is essential when it comes to your finances. Take the initiative to have meaningful conversations about your financial situation with your heirs. Inform them where you keep your money and provide them with information regarding the beneficiaries of all bank accounts and any life insurance policies you may have. By being transparent about your intentions and plans, you can avoid confusion or disputes in the future and ensure that your wishes are respected.

Schedule a family meeting or individual discussions with your heirs to discuss your financial arrangements. Share information about your assets, debts, and overall financial plan. Explain your reasoning behind the choices you've made, especially when it comes to designating beneficiaries. Encourage them to ask questions and seek clarification on any concerns they may have.

Streamline Financial Accounts

In the modern world, it's easy to accumulate a myriad of bank accounts and credit cards, each serving a different purpose. However, this can lead to unnecessary complexity and administrative burden. As part of your death cleaning process, consider consolidating your bank accounts and credit cards. By streamlining your financial accounts, you can simplify your financial management, reduce the risk of overlooking obligations, and gain a clearer understanding of your overall financial health.

Start by reviewing your bank accounts and credit cards. Determine which accounts are essential and serve your current financial needs. Consider closing unnecessary accounts to simplify your financial landscape. When choosing which accounts to keep, consider factors such as fees, interest rates, and the convenience of managing multiple accounts. Also, remember that closing accounts may impact your credit or FICO score. Consolidating your accounts may involve transferring funds from one account to another or closing accounts entirely. Take the necessary steps to ensure a smooth transition and remember to update any automatic payments or direct deposits with the new account information.

Minimizing Unnecessary Expenses and Subscriptions

In your fast-paced life, it's so easy to accumulate unnecessary expenses and subscriptions that drain your financial resources. Take a critical look at your monthly spending habits and identify areas where you may be able to cut costs—whether it is magazines, online streaming services, or other monthly service subscriptions. Cancel subscriptions that no longer bring value to your life and reassess your discretionary spending. By embracing a more minimalist approach to your finances, you can redirect your resources toward what truly matters and align your financial choices with your values.

Review your bank and credit card statements to identify recurring expenses and subscriptions. Consider whether each expense aligns with your current priorities and brings value to your life. Cancel any subscriptions that are no longer essential or no longer align with your interests. Evaluate your discretionary spending and identify areas where you can reduce or eliminate unnecessary expenses. This may involve making conscious choices about dining out, entertainment, or luxury purchases. By reevaluating your spending habits, you can redirect your financial resources toward experiences and causes that hold greater significance for you.

Understanding your finances is a vital step in leaving behind an uncluttered legacy. By assessing your financial situation, gathering relevant information, and seeking professional assistance when needed, you can gain clarity and peace of mind regarding our financial well-being.

II. Creating or Updating Your Will & Legal Documents

Often referred to as a last will and testament, a will specifies how your assets and possessions will be distributed after you die. It serves as a roadmap to ensure that your wishes are respected, your loved ones are provided for, and your legacy endures as you intended.

In this section, we will explore creating and updating wills, recognizing their importance in safeguarding your legacy and ensuring your final wishes are fulfilled. Whether you are starting from scratch or have an existing will that needs revision, we will guide you through the process step by step.

Recognizing the Importance of a Will to Protect Your Legacy

By carefully crafting a will, you gain the power to control how your assets are distributed among your beneficiaries. You can allocate specific items to individuals, designate financial resources for loved ones, and even support charitable causes close to your heart. Without a will, your estate may be subject to intestacy laws, and the distribution of your assets will be left in the hands of the legal system rather than your personal intentions.

Protecting Your Assets & Ensuring their Correct Distribution

One of the primary purposes of a will is to protect your assets and ensure they are distributed according to your wishes. Your assets may include real estate, investments, bank accounts, personal belongings, and sentimental items of value. By explicitly stating your desires within your will, you provide clear instructions on how these assets should be managed and divided.

Appointing Guardianship for Minor Children or Dependents

A will provides a vital opportunity to designate guardianship for parents or legal guardians of minor children or dependents. Should the unthinkable occur, the well-being and care of your children must be entrusted to someone who understands your values and can assume this significant responsibility.

By appointing a guardian within your will, you express your wishes regarding the individuals you believe would provide the most suitable environment for raising your children. While the ultimate decision rests with the courts, your expressed preference carries significant weight and serves as a guiding principle in their determination.

Consulting a Lawyer or Using Online Resources to Draft a Will

When creating or updating your will, you have several options available. One approach is to seek the guidance of a qualified lawyer specializing in estate planning. A legal professional can provide valuable insights, ensure compliance with local laws, and help you navigate complex financial considerations.

If engaging a lawyer is not feasible, or if you prefer a more independent route, you may consider using online resources to draft your will. Numerous reputable websites offer user-friendly platforms that guide you through the process step by step. These platforms typically provide templates, prompts, and explanations to help you understand the legal requirements and implications of each decision you make.

Updating the Will Periodically to Reflect Changing Circumstances

Once you have created your will, it is important to recognize that it is not a static document. Life is ever evolving, and as circumstances change, so too might your wishes regarding the distribution of your assets and the guardianship of your children.

It is advisable to review your will periodically, ideally at least once every few years, to ensure it accurately reflects your current intentions. Major life events such as marriage, divorce, birth, death, or changes in financial status should prompt a thorough review of your will. By taking a proactive approach and updating your will, you can maintain confidence that your legacy will be protected, and your wishes respected.

By recognizing the importance of a will, making sure it is up to date, protecting your assets, appointing guardianship, and seeking legal guidance, when necessary, you can navigate the intricate landscape of will creation with confidence. Whether you choose to consult a lawyer or utilize online resources, the key is to understand the legal requirements and implications while periodically reviewing and updating your will to reflect your changing circumstances.

By taking the time to craft a comprehensive and thoughtful will, you embrace the opportunity to shape your legacy and leave behind an uncluttered and intentional footprint on the world.

Other End-of Life-Documents

In addition to consulting an attorney about a will, you may wish to discuss a revocable living trust, financial power of attorney, a living will, or a medical power of attorney. These essential end-of-life documents can play a crucial role in ensuring your wishes are respected, and your loved ones are well taken care of when you're no longer able to make decisions for yourself.

Consult with the appropriate professional to answer questions about these documents. Some of these legal documents may also be available online from reputable companies such as LegalZoom.com.

III. Funeral Plans

When it comes to Swedish Death Cleaning, it is essential to address not only your finances but also how you want to be remembered. One such crucial aspect is planning your funeral arrangements. While death is a topic, many prefer to avoid or postpone considering it is a reality that awaits us all. By embracing the concept of Swedish Death Cleaning and applying its principles to our funeral plans, you can alleviate the burden on your loved ones and ensure that your final wishes are fulfilled.

The Significance of Pre-planning a Funeral

Death is an event that can often catch us off guard, leaving our families and friends in a state of shock and confusion. By taking the time to pre-plan our funeral, we are not only assuming responsibility for our own departure but also granting a sense of peace and direction to those we leave behind. Pre-planning a funeral allows us to make informed decisions, consider our options, and communicate our desires clearly. It is an opportunity to create a meaningful farewell that reflects our values, beliefs, and the life we have lived.

Communicating Your Funeral Plans with Loved Ones

One of the first steps in pre-planning your funeral is to openly communicate your wishes to your family members and close friends. Engage in honest conversations about your desires for the funeral ceremony, including your preferences for the type of service, location, and any specific rituals or customs you would like to be observed. By involving your loved ones in these discussions, you provide them with the opportunity to understand your wishes and support you in honoring them when the time comes.

It is important to emphasize that these conversations should take place in a supportive and understanding environment. Understand that your loved ones may have their own emotional responses to discussing your funeral plans, and it is crucial to approach these discussions with empathy and patience. Encourage open dialogue and assure them that your intention is to alleviate their burden and ensure that your final wishes are respected.

Documenting Your End-of-Life Choices

Once you have expressed your funeral ceremony wishes, it

is essential to document them in a clear and comprehensive manner. Create a written record that outlines the specifics of your desired funeral arrangements, including details about the type of service, readings, music, and any other elements that hold personal significance to you. Ensure that this document is stored securely and can be easily accessed by your designated loved ones or executor when needed. Consider sharing a copy with a trusted individual or storing it in a safe place, such as a safe deposit box.

Different Funeral Options

When planning your funeral, it is important to explore different options and choose the one that aligns with your values and beliefs. Traditional burial and cremation are the two most common choices, each offering its own unique considerations. Traditional burial involves interring the body in a cemetery, while cremation transforms the body into ashes, which can be stored in an urn, scattered, or used in other memorial options. Additionally, there are other options, such as full-body sea burials, scattering cremated remains at sea, or carbon-neutral human composting. Take the time to research and understand the cultural, religious, and environmental implications of these options and select the one that resonates with you the most.

If you choose a traditional burial, consider whether you want to be buried in a family plot or a separate gravesite. Explore different cemeteries in your area and consider their location, aesthetics, and any specific requirements or restrictions they may have. If you opt for cremation, think about how you would like your ashes to be handled. Some people choose to have their ashes scattered in a meaningful location, while others prefer to have them stored in an urn or incorporated into a memorial object.

Pre-paying for Cremation or Purchasing a Burial Plot

In addition to deciding between burial and cremation, it is also worth considering pre-paying for cremation services or purchasing a burial plot in advance. Pre-paying for cremation allows you to lock in current prices and potentially save your loved ones from the financial burden of arranging the service when the time comes. Similarly, purchasing a burial plot in advance ensures that your final resting place is secured according to your preferences. These considerations can help ease the logistical and financial strain on your family, allowing them to focus on grieving and celebrating your life instead.

When pre-paying for cremation services, research reputable providers in your area and carefully review their terms and conditions. Understand what services are included in the pre-payment plan and whether any additional costs may arise in the future. If you purchase a burial plot, visit different cemeteries to explore their options and pricing. Consider factors such as the location, maintenance, and long-term accessibility of the cemetery.

Planning for Your Funeral Ceremony

Beyond the decision of burial or cremation, there are various aspects to consider when planning the actual funeral ceremony. Think about the type of service you would like to have. Would you prefer a religious or secular ceremony? Are there any specific cultural or religious customs you would like to incorporate? Consider whether you would like a formal gathering or a more informal and intimate gathering of close friends and family.

Think about the venue for the funeral ceremony. It could be held at a religious institution, a funeral home, or even a location that holds personal significance to you, such as a park or a beach. Ensure that the chosen venue can accommodate the number of attendees you anticipate and that it aligns with the desired atmosphere and tone of the ceremony.

In addition to the overall structure of the ceremony, consider the specific elements that will make it meaningful and reflective of your life. Choose readings, poems, or religious passages that resonate with you and capture your essence. Select music that holds personal significance, or that represents your favorite songs or genres. If you have any specific requests for rituals or customs to be observed, communicate them clearly to your loved ones or include them in your documented funeral plans.

It is important to remember that funeral ceremonies are not only a time for mourning but also an opportunity to celebrate the life and memories of the person who has passed away. Consider whether you would like to incorporate elements of celebration or remembrance into the ceremony. This could include sharing anecdotes, displaying photographs or videos, or organizing activities that reflect your interests and passions.

Death is a part of life, and although it may be uncomfortable to confront, it is better to face it head-on. By integrating funeral planning into the framework of Swedish Death Cleaning, we can embrace the inevitability of death and ensure that our wishes are respected and fulfilled. Through clear communication, documentation, and consideration of different options, we empower ourselves and our loved ones to approach this final chapter of life with grace, preparedness, and a sense of purpose.

By taking responsibility for our funeral plans, we leave an uncluttered legacy that not only lightens the load for those we leave behind but also allows them to celebrate our lives and memories without the weight of uncertainty. Let us approach the subject of death with openness and wisdom, knowing that our preparations will serve as a loving gift to those we cherish most.

Step 4 Conclusion

In this step, we explored an often-overlooked aspect of Swedish Death Cleaning—the importance of organizing finances, creating a will, and making funeral plans. By embracing the concept of Swedish Death Cleaning and actively engaging in organizing our finances, creating a will, and making funeral plans, we can experience a profound sense of accomplishment and satisfaction. In the next step, we will transition from discussing the practical benefits of Swedish Death Cleaning and delve into the profound wisdom behind this process.

Step 5. The Power of Simplicity & Minimalism

In the preceding sections of this book, we embarked on a journey to declutter our physical environment, organize our belongings, and make deliberate choices about what we hold onto and what we let go. As we dig deeper into the transformative wisdom of Swedish Death Cleaning, we reach a critical juncture where practicality converges with philosophy and wisdom.

Steps 1 to 4 provided us with the necessary tools to declutter our external environment and establish harmony in our lives. The remaining chapters of this book will be dedicated to organizing our internal realm, encompassing our psychological, emotional, and spiritual aspects.

I. Expanding Your Inner Life Through Simplicity & Minimalism

Many individuals are seeking ways to unburden themselves from the overwhelming clutter and chaos that permeates their lives. In this section, we explore the profound wisdom behind these practices, offering insights on how to embrace simplicity and minimalism to unclutter every aspect of our lives and find deeper meaning and purpose.

Simplicity involves stripping away the excess, both in our physical surroundings and our mental and emotional states. It encourages us to identify and prioritize what truly matters to us, allowing us to live in alignment with our core values. Minimalism, on the other hand, urges us to consciously curate our possessions, relationships, and commitments, ensuring that each one adds value and meaning to our lives. By gaining a deeper understanding of simplicity and minimalism, we can begin to unlock their transformative power.

One of the critical benefits of simplicity and minimalism in the external world is the benefit this practice has on our internal world—our inner space. When we are distracted by the disorganization of life, we sometimes find it difficult to look inward, which is where the richness of our life dwells. In an increasingly busy and distracted world, creating physical and mental space allows us to connect with ourselves on a deeper level.

By decluttering our physical environment, we remove distractions and create a tranquil atmosphere that promotes clarity and focus. Similarly, by decluttering our mental and emotional space, we free ourselves from the burdens of excessive thoughts and attachments, enabling us to explore our true desires, passions, and aspirations. This section explores how simplicity and minimalism provide fertile ground for personal growth, helping us rediscover our authentic selves and find renewed purpose and meaning.

Understanding Simplicity and Minimalism

While simplicity and minimalism share the common goal of leading a more intentional and fulfilling life, they differ in their approaches and emphasis. Simplicity is primarily concerned with reducing complexity and embracing a straightforward lifestyle, while minimalism focuses on living with fewer possessions and eliminating excess. Let us delve deeper into each concept, exploring their characteristics, benefits, and how they can be applied to unclutter our lives and find meaning and purpose.

Simplicity is about cutting through the noise and finding clarity in our lives. It involves streamlining our routines, eliminating unnecessary complications, and prioritizing what truly matters to us. Simplicity encourages us to reflect on our values and goals, enabling us to make conscious choices that align with our authentic selves. By simplifying our lives, we create space for what is truly important, whether spending time with loved ones, pursuing meaningful work, or engaging in activities that bring us joy and fulfillment.

One aspect of simplicity is simplifying our physical environment. This entails decluttering our homes and getting rid of items we no longer need or cherish. By letting go of excess possessions, we free ourselves from the burden of managing and maintaining them. This process not only helps us create a more organized and visually pleasing space but also allows us to appreciate and value the items we choose to keep. Simplicity in our physical surroundings can lead to a sense of calmness, making it easier to focus on what truly matters and reducing distractions that hinder our well-being.

Moreover, simplicity extends beyond our physical environment and into our mental, emotional, and spiritual realms. It encourages us to simplify our thoughts, priorities, and commitments. By decluttering our minds, we create mental space for reflection, creativity, and problem-solving. Simplifying our commitments involves being selective about how we spend our time and energy, saying no to activities and obligations that do not align with our values or contribute positively to our lives. This allows us to allocate our resources more effectively, fostering a greater sense of control and purpose.

In contrast, minimalism emphasizes living with fewer possessions and embracing a minimalist lifestyle. Minimalism challenges the notion that material possessions equate to happiness and encourages us to question our consumerist habits. It advocates for intentional consumption, where we only acquire or keep items that serve a purpose or bring genuine joy. By adopting a minimalist mindset, we shift our focus from accumulating possessions to cultivating relationships, experiences, personal growth, and overall well-being.

Minimalism invites us to evaluate our attachment to material possessions and recognize the emotional and psychological burden that excessive consumerism can create. Often, the pursuit of more possessions leads to a never-ending cycle of desire and dissatisfaction. By consciously choosing to live with fewer things, we can break free from this cycle and discover contentment in a life driven by experiences rather than material accumulation.

Living a minimalist lifestyle also aligns with environmental sustainability. By reducing our consumption, we decrease our ecological footprint and contribute to a more sustainable future. Minimalism encourages us to consider the impact of our choices on the environment and make conscious decisions that prioritize conservation and mindful consumption.

While simplicity and minimalism differ in their emphasis, they are interconnected concepts that complement each other. Simplifying our lives by reducing complexity and focusing on what truly matters paves the way for minimalism to thrive. Simplicity provides the foundation upon which minimalism can be built, as it involves decluttering and streamlining our physical and mental spaces. By embracing simplicity, we create the necessary mindset and environment to adopt a minimalist lifestyle successfully.

Both simplicity and minimalism offer numerous benefits beyond the mere act of decluttering. They can lead to increased mindfulness, improved well-being, enhanced creativity, and stronger relationships. By removing distractions and excess from our lives, we open up space and time for self-reflection, personal growth, and pursuing our passions.

It is important to note that simplicity and minimalism are personal journeys, and the extent to which we embrace these concepts may vary from person to person. What works for one individual may not work for another, as our values, circumstances, and preferences differ. The key is to find a balance that resonates with our unique needs and aspirations.

The Benefits of Cultivating Inner Space

By cultivating inner space through simplicity and minimalism, we open ourselves up to numerous benefits that positively impact our well-being and overall quality of life:

Enhanced Mental Clarity

A cluttered physical environment often leads to a cluttered mind. When we simplify our surroundings, we create a calmer mental landscape, allowing us to think more clearly and make better decisions. Clearing physical clutter not only removes distractions but also frees up mental space, enabling us to focus on what truly matters to us.

Reduced Stress

The demands of modern life can leave us feeling overwhelmed, constantly juggling multiple responsibilities and commitments. Embracing minimalism helps us let go of excess possessions, responsibilities, and commitments, thereby reducing stress and allowing us to focus on what truly matters. By intentionally simplifying our lives, we create a sense of balance and regain control over our time and energy.

Increased Freedom & Flexibility

Owning fewer possessions and attachments grants us a sense of freedom and flexibility. We are no longer burdened by the weight of material possessions, and we have more time, energy, and resources to pursue our passions and live life on our own terms. Minimalism allows us to break free from the consumerist mindset and find liberation in experiences and relationships rather than in the accumulation of things.

Heightened Appreciation for the Present

Simplifying our lives enables us to be more present and fully engaged in the moment. When we let go of unnecessary distractions and focus on the essentials, we can savor the richness of everyday experiences. By cultivating inner space, we develop a deeper appreciation for the simple joys of life, fostering gratitude and contentment.

Cultivating inner space is not a one-time task but an ongoing journey. It requires a shift in mindset and a commitment to continuous evaluation and intentional living. It involves developing a deeper understanding of our values, priorities, and the impact our choices have on our well-being and the world around us. By embracing simplicity and minimalism, we embark on a transformative path that extends beyond our immediate environment and permeates various aspects of our lives.

In essence, simplicity and minimalism are transformative practices that enable us to shift our focus from the external accumulation of material possessions to the internal cultivation of a rich and meaningful life. By embracing the power of simplicity and minimalism, we embark on a journey toward greater contentment, authenticity, and fulfillment.

II. The Psychological, Emotional, & Spiritual Impact of Living with Less

In a world that often equates happiness with material wealth and accumulation, the concept of living with less may seem counterintuitive. However, there is a growing movement embracing minimalism and simplicity to find true contentment and inner peace. By shedding excess and prioritizing what truly matters, individuals can experience a profound psychological, emotional, and spiritual transformation.

Living with less allows individuals to break free from the constant pursuit of possessions and societal expectations, which often lead to stress, anxiety, and dissatisfaction. By reducing clutter and eliminating unnecessary distractions, the mind becomes clearer and more focused. This newfound mental clarity can alleviate feelings of overwhelm and create a sense of calmness and tranquility.

Furthermore, minimalism encourages individuals to cultivate a deeper connection with themselves and their surroundings. With fewer material possessions to define their identity, people are prompted to explore their true values, passions, and purpose. This introspection leads to a heightened self-awareness and a greater sense of authenticity.

Exploring the Emotional Weight Associated with Excessive Belongings

Many of us have experienced the weight of excessive belongings in our lives. Our possessions can become burdens rather than sources of joy for us. Cluttered spaces can overwhelm our senses, leading to feelings of anxiety and stress. The emotional weight associated with excessive belongings goes beyond the physical realm; it also affects our mental and emotional well-being.

Psychologically, clutter can create a sense of chaos and disorder in our minds. It becomes a constant reminder of unfinished tasks and unmet expectations. The more possessions we accumulate, the more energy and attention we need to invest in managing and maintaining them. This can lead to a cycle of stress and dissatisfaction as we become trapped in a never-ending quest for more.

Emotionally, excessive belongings can also hinder our ability to let go. We may develop attachments to material possessions, associating them with memories, identities, or aspirations. Letting go of these possessions can feel like letting go of a part of ourselves. However, by examining the emotional weight associated with excessive belongings, we can start to question the true value they bring to our lives.

Finding Liberation & Contentment in Detaching from Materialism

Living with less offers a path to liberation and contentment. By consciously choosing to detach from materialism, we free ourselves from the constant pursuit of possessions and external validation. We shift our focus from accumulating things to nurturing relationships, experiences, and personal growth.

When we let go of the attachment to material possessions, we create space in our lives for more meaningful experiences. We can redirect our energy toward activities that bring us joy, such as pursuing hobbies, spending time in nature, or connecting with loved ones. As we detach from the need for material objects to define our worth, we discover that true contentment comes from within.

Living with less also allows us to cultivate a greater sense of gratitude. By intentionally reducing our possessions, we become more aware of what we have and appreciate the abundance already present in our lives. Gratitude has been linked to numerous psychological benefits, including increased happiness, improved relationships, and enhanced overall well-being.

Deepening Connections with Oneself & Others

Living with less provides an opportunity to deepen our connections with ourselves and others. When we are not constantly distracted by material possessions, we can turn our attention inward and engage in self-reflection. We can gain a clearer understanding of our values, desires, and passions, leading to a stronger sense of self-awareness and authenticity.

By detaching from materialism, we also create more space for meaningful relationships. Instead of focusing on acquiring possessions, we can invest our time and energy in nurturing connections with others. Meaningful relationships are essential for our well-being and can provide support, love, and a sense of belonging. Living with less allows us to prioritize these relationships and foster deeper connections with the people who truly matter to us.

By simplifying our lives, we create more opportunities for meaningful experiences. We can allocate our resources, both time and money, toward activities that align with our values and bring us joy. Whether traveling, pursuing creative endeavors, or engaging in community service, we can cultivate a life rich in experiences rather than possessions.

Living with less also allows us to make a positive impact on the environment and contribute to a more sustainable future. By reducing our consumption and embracing minimalism, we decrease our carbon footprint and promote a lifestyle that values quality over quantity. This conscious choice to live with less can bring a sense of purpose and fulfillment as we contribute to a healthier planet for future generations.

The Spiritual Impact of Minimalism

The profound spiritual impact of embracing minimalism cannot be overstated. When individuals choose to detach themselves from the allure of material possessions, they embark on a transformative journey that redirects their focus toward the intangible aspects of life. By shedding the unnecessary clutter and distractions that often consume our attention, minimalism opens up the space for individuals to nurture relationships, seek meaningful experiences, and embark on a journey of personal growth. In this process, a deeper appreciation for the present moment is cultivated, and a profound connection to something greater than oneself is forged. Whether through the practice of meditation, the cultivation of mindfulness, or the rediscovery of our innate connection to nature, minimalism has the power to foster a spiritual awakening and a heightened sense of interconnectedness.

At the core of minimalism lies the idea that true fulfillment and contentment do not arise from the accumulation of material possessions. Instead, minimalism prompts individuals to explore the depths of their own being and discover the richness that lies within. By detaching from the constant desire for more and the relentless pursuit of external validation, individuals can redirect their attention toward inner exploration and personal reflection. This process encourages a shift from a materialistic mindset to a more mindful and intentional way of living.

One of the fundamental practices that often accompanies minimalism is meditation. Through the act of sitting in stillness and quieting the mind, individuals can delve into the depths of their consciousness and connect with their inner selves. This practice cultivates a heightened sense of self-awareness and allows individuals to observe their thoughts, emotions, and desires without judgment. By witnessing these aspects of the self, individuals gain a deeper understanding of their own inner workings and develop a greater sense of clarity and purpose.

Mindfulness, another integral aspect of minimalism, involves consciously engaging with the present moment and fully immersing oneself in the here and now. By embracing mindfulness, individuals can break free from the constant distractions and mental chatter that often dominate their lives. Instead, they can cultivate a state of focused attention and heightened awareness. This heightened state of consciousness enables individuals to fully appreciate the beauty and wonder that exist in even the simplest of experiences. Whether it is savoring the taste of a delicious meal, feeling the warmth of the sun on their skin, or marveling at the intricate details of nature, mindfulness allows individuals to experience a profound sense of awe and wonder for the present moment.

Moreover, minimalism provides an opportunity to reconnect with nature, the ultimate source of inspiration and interconnectedness. By simplifying one's surroundings and creating a space that is in harmony with nature, individuals can experience a deep sense of peace and tranquility. Spending time in nature allows individuals to reconnect with the rhythms and cycles of life, reminding them of their place within the larger web of existence. Whether it is taking a leisurely walk in the woods, gazing at a starry sky, or feeling the soothing embrace of the ocean, nature has the power to awaken a sense of reverence and awe within individuals.

The spiritual impact of minimalism is profound and transformative. By detaching from material possessions and embracing a more intentional and mindful way of living, individuals can cultivate a deeper appreciation for the present moment and a heightened sense of interconnectedness. Through practices such as meditation, mindfulness, and a renewed connection with nature, individuals can embark on a spiritual journey of self-discovery and inner growth. Minimalism offers a path toward a more meaningful and fulfilling existence, one that transcends the confines of material wealth and connects us to something greater than ourselves.

Step 5 Conclusion

In this step, we explored the concept of cultivating inner space through simplicity and minimalism, understanding the power of decluttering our physical environment and its impact on our mental, emotional, and spiritual well-being. In the next step, we will explore the reality that everything in life is temporary, including ourselves.

Step 6. Everything is Temporary

Everything is temporary. Every thought, every emotion, every possession, every relationship, and even our own lives have a birth and death cycle. In our life's journey, we are invited to explore the profound notion that every facet of life is transient, including our own existence. The concept of impermanence can evoke both discomfort and liberation within us. However, by wholeheartedly embracing this truth, we open ourselves up to a profound and deeper understanding of ourselves and the intricate world we inhabit. As we acknowledge and accept the transient nature of all things, we can embark on a path toward discovering renewed purpose and profound meaning in our lives.

Our human tendency often leads us to seek stability,

permanence, and security. We cling to possessions, relationships, and experiences, yearning for a sense of certainty and control. We get stressed out when things change, when relationships end, and when our health begins to fail. Yet, the truth is that life is an ever-changing tapestry of experiences, emotions, and circumstances. Nothing remains static or eternal. The sooner we recognize and come to terms with this fundamental truth, the more we can liberate ourselves from the burdensome weight of attachment and expectations.

Embracing impermanence requires a shift in perspective—a gentle revolution within our minds and hearts. It challenges us to confront our mortality, reminding us that our time on this Earth is limited and fragile. Rather than being disheartened by this realization, we can harness its power to propel us toward a life of greater authenticity, purpose, and connection.

By embracing the transitory nature of life, we develop a profound appreciation for the present moment. We begin to cherish the beauty in fleeting experiences, recognizing that each passing second is an opportunity for growth and self-discovery. The impermanence of life urges us to savor the joyous moments, to relish the deep connections we forge, and to cherish the memories we create along the way.

Moreover, embracing impermanence allows us to release the grip of material possessions that often clutter our lives and distract us from what truly matters. As we understand that the accumulation of objects is merely a temporary pursuit, we become more discerning in our choices, valuing quality over quantity and focusing on possessions that align with our values and bring genuine joy.

As we embark on this section, let us embrace the uncertainty and imperfection inherent in life. Let us navigate the ever-changing tides with an open heart and a curious mind, knowing each moment presents an opportunity for introspection and growth. By relinquishing our attachment to the illusion of permanence, we invite a profound transformation that reverberates through every aspect of our being.

I. Impermanence & Mortality as Essential Aspects of Life

As we progress on our Swedish Death Cleaning journey, we confront a universal and deeply personal truth—the reality of impermanence and mortality. Impermanence, the fact that everything is temporary, refers to the ever-changing nature of existence. It reminds us that nothing remains the same, and everything we encounter—people, relationships, experiences—will eventually end. Mortality, on the other hand, is the acknowledgment of our finite lifespan and the inevitability of death.

In its essence, part of accepting life and accepting reality is about coming to terms with the undeniable fact that everything in life is transient and fleeting. From the material possessions we accumulate to the physical spaces we occupy, nothing is permanent. This realization may initially evoke uncomfortable feelings, as we are inherently wired to seek stability and permanence. However, by embracing the impermanence of our existence, we can find freedom and liberation from the burden of attachment.

Mortality, though often considered a morbid topic, is a powerful catalyst for living a purposeful life. When we confront our own mortality, we are prompted to examine our priorities and question the legacy we wish to leave behind. We are reminded of our limited time and the importance of making the most of it. Embracing our mortality inspires us to pursue our passions, nurture our relationships, and contribute meaningfully to the world.

While impermanence and mortality are distinct concepts, they share a fundamental connection. Impermanence is a broader concept encompassing all aspects of existence, while mortality refers explicitly to the inevitability of death. Mortality is a reminder of our limited time on Earth, emphasizing the fragility and transience of life. It is the ultimate manifestation of impermanence, as death is the ultimate change that awaits every living being.

Impermanence and mortality can be seen as two sides of the same coin. Impermanence highlights the ever-changing nature of existence, whereas mortality focuses on the finite nature of human life. Understanding impermanence prepares us for the reality of mortality and enables us to embrace the transient nature of our existence. By recognizing that everything is impermanent, including our own lives, we can develop a sense of urgency to live fully and meaningfully.

While impermanence and mortality share similarities, they also have distinct characteristics and implications. Impermanence applies to all phenomena, whereas mortality is specific to living beings. Impermanence encompasses both the macrocosm and microcosm, encompassing galaxies, civilizations, and individual lives, while mortality pertains only to the human experience.

Impermanence can be observed in the cycle of seasons, the rise and fall of civilizations, the aging of our bodies, and the changing dynamics of relationships. It reminds us that nothing is exempt from change and that clinging to things as they are will inevitably lead to suffering. On the other hand, mortality directly confronts us with the finiteness of our time on Earth, urging us to reflect on the choices we make and the legacy we leave behind.

One significant distinction between impermanence and mortality lies in their temporal scale. Impermanence encompasses both the immediate changes we experience in our daily lives and the grander shifts that occur over longer periods. Mortality, however, is a singular event—the end of one's life. While impermanence can be observed and contemplated throughout life, mortality becomes particularly salient as we approach our own death or face the loss of loved ones.

Recognizing impermanence and mortality as essential aspects of life can have profound implications for our attitudes, behaviors, and overall well-being. Embracing impermanence helps us let go of attachments and expectations, fostering a sense of freedom and flexibility. Our awareness of impermanence allows us to appreciate the present moment, knowing that it will never be the same again.

Understanding mortality can catalyze prioritizing what truly matters in our lives. It prompts us to reflect on our values, relationships, and the legacy we want to leave behind. By acknowledging our mortality, we gain clarity about the transient nature of material possessions and shift our focus toward more meaningful experiences and connections.

Embracing impermanence and mortality also cultivates gratitude and mindfulness. When we acknowledge that everything is temporary, we can savor the beauty and joys of life while they last. We become more present and engaged, knowing that each moment is a gift that will never come again.

Moreover, accepting impermanence and mortality can alleviate anxiety and fear. By realizing that change is inevitable, and death is a natural part of life, we can find solace and peace in the face of uncertainty. It allows us to navigate life's challenges with resilience and adaptability, knowing that even difficult circumstances will eventually pass.

Impermanence and mortality are intrinsic aspects of life that shape our existence in profound ways. Embracing impermanence helps us recognize the transient nature of all things, encouraging us to live with intention, appreciation, and acceptance. Mortality, on the other hand, confronts us with the finiteness of our time on Earth, inspiring us to reflect on our priorities and make the most of the limited time we have.

We can find greater meaning, purpose, and fulfillment by understanding and accepting impermanence and mortality. We can approach life with a sense of urgency and seize each opportunity for growth, connection, and self-discovery. Ultimately, embracing impermanence and mortality allows us to live authentically and leave a lasting legacy of love, compassion, and wisdom.

II. Embracing Impermanence

In our journey through life, we often find ourselves clinging to things, people, and experiences. We yearn for permanence, stability, and security. However, the truth is that everything in life is temporary. The mantra "everything is temporary" reminds us of this fundamental truth. It serves as a powerful reminder that life is a continuous cycle of creation, destruction, and transformation.

When we deeply understand and internalize the concept of impermanence, it can bring us great liberation. Rather than resisting the natural flow of life, we learn to embrace it. We realize that change is the only constant, and instead of fearing it, we can find peace and meaning in accepting it.

Swedish Death Cleaning recognizes and embraces the impermanence of our possessions and physical spaces. It prompts us to confront the reality that one day, we will leave everything behind. By accepting this truth, we can approach the process of decluttering with a renewed sense of purpose and intention. It is not merely about getting rid of unnecessary items but rather about consciously choosing what truly matters and cultivating a meaningful life.

Embracing impermanence does not mean disregarding the importance of things or relationships in our lives. On the contrary, it allows us to cherish and value them even more. When we recognize that everything is temporary, we appreciate the present moment with greater mindfulness and gratitude. We savor the joys and find solace in the sorrows, knowing they, too, shall pass.

The Manta "Everything is Temporary"
The mantra "everything is temporary" teaches us the art of acceptance. It invites us to surrender to the natural rhythm of life rather than resisting or clinging to what is passing. By embracing impermanence, we cultivate resilience and

flexibility. We learn to adapt to changing circumstances with grace and openness.

In the face of loss, whether it be the end of a relationship, the passing of a loved one, or the transition from one phase of life to another, accepting the impermanence of it all can be immensely healing. It allows us to grieve, let go, and eventually find the strength to move forward. By acknowledging that everything is temporary, we create space for new possibilities to emerge.

Moreover, embracing the ebb and flow of life helps us navigate the challenges that arise. Difficult moments become less overwhelming when we remind ourselves that they are fleeting and part of a greater tapestry. Just as the waves of the ocean rise and fall, so do our experiences.

The mantra acts as a compass, guiding us through the ups and downs and reminding us to stay grounded in the present and maintain perspective. In our fast-paced and often chaotic world, overwhelming moments can easily consume us. We may feel weighed down by stress, anxiety, or the weight of responsibilities. However, the mantra "everything is temporary" acts as a beacon of light in those dark times.

When we repeat this mantra to ourselves, we create a mental

space that allows us to step back and gain clarity. It helps us recognize that the challenges we face are fleeting and that we have the inner strength to endure and transcend them. By acknowledging the impermanence of our difficulties, we loosen their grip on our minds and find a sense of liberation.

The mantra also encourages us to let go of attachments and expectations. We often suffer when we cling to specific outcomes or resist the natural unfolding of events. By reminding ourselves that everything is temporary, we free ourselves from the need for control and surrender to the flow of life. This surrender brings peace, resilience, and a renewed sense of purpose.

Moreover, the mantra helps us cultivate a deeper appreciation for the present moment. When we realize everything is transient, we become more fully present in our daily lives. We savor simple joys, express gratitude for our blessings, and cultivate a greater awareness of the beauty and fragility of life.

Life experiences are inherently transient. We go through moments of joy, sorrow, success, and failure, but they all pass by like fleeting clouds in the sky. When we recognize this impermanence, we can fully immerse ourselves in the present moment, cherishing the experiences as they arise without clinging to them. The impermanence of relationships becomes evident too. People come and go, and friendships evolve or fade away. Understanding that relationships are ever-changing allows us to appreciate the connections we have in the here and now, making the most of the time we spend with loved ones.

Possessions, too, have a transient nature. Material goods come into our lives, serve a purpose, and eventually depart. Whether it's an old piece of furniture or a cherished memento, everything eventually wears out, breaks, or loses significance. Recognizing this impermanence helps us detach from our possessions and find freedom from the burden of accumulating more than we need. By acknowledging that material possessions are temporary, we can focus on what truly matters: the experiences and relationships that bring meaning to our lives.

The Benefits of Embracing Impermanence

When we accept impermanence, we become more aware of the beauty and preciousness of each moment. Instead of taking things for granted, we develop a deep sense of gratitude for the people and experiences that enrich our lives. Every sunset, every shared laugh, and every heartfelt conversation becomes a gift to be cherished. By cultivating gratitude, we shift our focus from what we lack to what we have, leading to greater contentment and fulfillment.

Attachment is a natural human tendency, but it can also bring about suffering. When we cling to relationships, experiences, or possessions, we create expectations and build our happiness on the condition that they remain unchanged. However, the reality of impermanence disrupts these expectations. By embracing impermanence, we learn to let go and release our attachments. We no longer rely on external factors for our well-being and find greater inner peace. The fear of loss and the pain of separation are eased, allowing us to navigate life's changes with equanimity.

Embracing impermanence opens the door to personal growth and resilience. When we acknowledge that change is an inherent part of life, we become more adaptable and open-minded. We learn to embrace new experiences, recognizing that they contribute to our growth and transformation. By accepting impermanence, we develop resilience in the face of challenges. We understand that difficult times are temporary, and they, too, shall pass. This perspective empowers us to navigate adversity with strength and determination.

Embracing impermanence is a profound shift in mindset that can bring immense benefits to our lives. By recognizing the transient nature of life relationships, experiences, and possessions, we can cultivate gratitude, relieve attachment, and foster personal growth and resilience. Embracing impermanence allows us to live more fully in the present moment, appreciating the beauty and richness that life offers. So, let us embrace impermanence and find meaning and purpose in the ever-changing tapestry of our existence.

III. Facing Our Mortality

In our modern society, the topic of death is often avoided or brushed aside as if it were a taboo subject. We go about our daily lives, distracted by the hustle and bustle, refusing to acknowledge the inevitable reality that awaits us all. This denial of death is a defense mechanism—a psychological coping mechanism that allows us to distance ourselves from the uncomfortable thoughts and feelings associated with our mortality.

The Common Tendency to Deny Our Mortality

The denial of death is deeply ingrained in human nature, woven into the very fabric of our existence. It is a psychological defense mechanism that shields us from the harsh reality that our lives are finite, and that death is an inevitable part of the human experience. Facing our mortality can be an overwhelming and unsettling prospect, stirring up existential questions that challenge our sense of identity, purpose, and the meaning of life itself. Consequently, we often resort to various strategies and coping mechanisms to avoid directly confronting the impending inevitability of our own demise.

One way we navigate this fundamental dilemma is by constructing elaborate narratives and belief systems that provide comfort and reassurance. These narratives, often rooted in religious, spiritual, or philosophical traditions, offer explanations about the nature of life, death, and what lies beyond. They present concepts of immortality, reincarnation, or an afterlife, offering solace and a sense of continuity beyond the boundaries of earthly existence. By embracing these beliefs, we create a shield against the raw and unsettling reality of our own mortality, finding solace in the hope that there is something more awaiting us on the other side.

While there is nothing inherently wrong with embracing a belief system that answers life's deepest questions, it is important to acknowledge that, at times, these deeply held convictions can divert our attention from fully experiencing the present moment in the here and now. Consequently, they may inadvertently lead us to pass judgment on individuals who hold differing beliefs, which is often contrary to our religious beliefs in the first place.

While faith can provide solace, guidance, and a sense of purpose, it is crucial to strike a balance between our spiritual convictions and our ability to remain open-minded and respectful toward others. In the pursuit of eternal truths, we must recognize the potential for our beliefs to cloud our perception of the world around us.

By fixating on the eternal nature of our faith, we might inadvertently overlook the beauty and richness of the present moment. Our preoccupation with the afterlife or future rewards can hinder our ability to fully engage with the people and experiences that shape our lives here and now. It is in the present moment that we have the opportunity to form genuine connections, learn from diverse perspectives, and cultivate empathy for those who hold beliefs different from our own.

Similarly, when we turn a blind eye to the challenges right in front of us, hoping that our circumstances will miraculously improve someday, we waste the precious problem-solving abilities bestowed upon us by God. These inherent gifts, meant to empower us to improve our own lives and the lives of others, lie dormant and untapped when we choose to ignore the problems that require our attention. While we may label this as having faith and trusting in a higher power it is really an act of irresponsibility. It is far better to do what you can in the present moment and ask for God's help and wisdom rather than sit on the sidelines waiting for God to do all the heavy lifting.

By disregarding the issues that confront us, we deny ourselves the opportunity for growth and progress. Instead of proactively addressing these challenges head-on, we choose to remain passive observers, hoping for a better tomorrow without taking any tangible steps to bring about change. In doing so, we underestimate our own capacity to tackle obstacles and create meaningful transformations.

Each of us possesses a unique combination of intellect, creativity, and resilience—a divine inheritance that equips us with the ability to confront and overcome the trials that life presents. It is through the utilization of these God-given problem-solving gifts that we can break free from the chains of complacency and forge a path toward a brighter future.

When we dismiss the difficulties that surround us, we not only hinder our own personal growth but also neglect our duty to uplift those around us. Our problem-solving abilities are not solely meant for self-improvement; they hold immense potential to make a positive impact on the lives of others. By embracing the challenges we encounter and applying our innate problem-solving gifts, we have the power to create ripples of change that extend far beyond ourselves.

When we acknowledge the problems before us, summon our God-given problem-solving abilities, and take decisive action, we embark on a journey of self-discovery and empowerment. By using these gifts to confront obstacles head-on, we demonstrate our faith in our own potential and recognize that we are not passive victims of circumstance but active agents of change.

Let us embrace the responsibility to address the problems we face, both personally and collectively, and utilize the divine problem-solving gifts that have been bestowed upon us. In doing so, we can transcend the limitations of our current circumstances and manifest a future filled with growth, progress, and the betterment of ourselves and those around us.

Moreover, when our faith becomes rigid and exclusive, it can breed a tendency to pass judgment on those who do not share our beliefs. This judgment may manifest as intolerance, discrimination, or even hostility toward others. Rather than appreciating the diversity of human experience and the multitude of paths people take in their spiritual journeys, we might fall into the trap of labeling and categorizing individuals based on their beliefs.

It is important to remember that every person has their own unique set of experiences, cultural influences, and personal beliefs that shape their worldview. By acknowledging and embracing this diversity, we can foster a greater understanding and acceptance of others. This does not mean compromising our own convictions, but rather cultivating a mindset of compassion, empathy, and respect that transcends the boundaries of belief systems.

Confronting our mortality can be an arduous and transformative journey. It requires us to acknowledge our vulnerability, embrace the impermanence of our existence, and grapple with the profound uncertainty that accompanies our mortality. By recognizing and accepting the fragility of life, we can develop a deeper appreciation for the present moment and the relationships and experiences that truly matter. Embracing our mortality doesn't mean dwelling on the negative but rather acknowledging the finite nature of our lives as a catalyst for living with greater intention and purpose.

The Potential Harm of Denying Death

By denying our mortality, we can easily lose sight of what truly matters in life. We become preoccupied with trivial matters, material possessions, and societal expectations, often neglecting our personal goals, passions, and relationships. Postponing the making of important life choices, such as pursuing our dreams or spending quality time with loved ones, becomes a common occurrence under the false assumption that there will always be time in the future. However, when we deny death, we fail to recognize the limited nature of our existence and the urgency to make the most of the time we have.

One of the fundamental dangers of denying death is the potential for wasting our lives on trivial matters. By ignoring the fact that our time on this earth is limited, we tend to prioritize insignificant things that hold no long-term value. Our focus shifts towards material possessions, as we seek happiness and fulfillment through the accumulation of wealth and goods. Consumerism becomes the center of our lives, replacing the pursuit of personal growth and true fulfillment.

Imagine waking up one day and realizing that you have become a caretaker of belongings instead of a dreamer of dreams. Without even realizing it, so many people give up on their childhood goals and aspirations to become a curator of things. Becoming ensnared in the relentless cycle of time and consumerism can reduce even the most remarkable individuals to mere slaves of materialism.

Additionally, societal expectations exert a powerful influence on our lives. We may feel pressured to conform to certain societal norms and ideals, sacrificing our authenticity and personal values in the process. The fear of mortality can drive us to pursue societal markers of success, such as wealth, status, and recognition, even if these pursuits do not align with our true desires and aspirations. As a result, we may find ourselves living a life that is inauthentic and unfulfilling, devoid of true purpose and meaning.

Paradoxically, the denial of death can also lead to an underlying sense of fear and anxiety. Deep down, we may sense the fleeting nature of life, but by refusing to confront it, we create a sense of unease that lingers beneath the surface. We may find ourselves constantly worrying about the unknown, the uncertainty, and the inevitability of our own mortality. This fear can manifest in various ways, affecting our mental and emotional well-being and preventing us from fully embracing and enjoying the present moment.

When we deny death, we suppress our innate human capacity for acceptance and resilience. We may become fixated on controlling every aspect of our lives, desperately seeking a sense of permanence and security. This constant need for control can lead to heightened anxiety as we try to navigate the unpredictable nature of life. We may develop an excessive fear of change and loss, hindering our ability to adapt and grow in the face of life's challenges.

Moreover, denying death can also breed a fear of aging. Society often perpetuates a negative view of aging, associating it with decline, loss of beauty, and diminished capabilities. When we deny death, we resist the natural aging process, clinging to youth and desperately attempting to defy the passage of time. This fear of aging can result in a constant state of dissatisfaction and self-judgment as we strive to meet unrealistic standards of appearance and physical vitality. We may become trapped in a cycle of seeking external validation and approval, constantly comparing ourselves to others and feeling inadequate as we age.

By denying death, we miss out on the profound opportunities for personal growth and self-reflection that arise from acknowledging our impermanence. When we confront the reality of our mortality, we are forced to reevaluate our lives, question our priorities, and consider the legacy we want to leave behind. This introspection can lead to transformative insights and a deeper understanding of ourselves. Without embracing our mortality, we may pass through life without ever truly knowing who we are or what we want to accomplish.

Acknowledging the transient nature of life allows us to approach each day with a sense of purpose and intention. It encourages us to prioritize our values and align our actions with what truly matters to us. Rather than mindlessly pursuing societal expectations or external validation, we can cultivate a life that is meaningful and authentic. We can focus on nurturing our relationships, pursuing our passions, and making a positive impact on the world around us.

The Benefits of Facing Our Mortality

When we confront the inevitability of death, it awakens within us a sense of urgency and motivation. We realize that time is a precious resource, and we become more determined to make the most of it. Embracing our mortality compels us to set meaningful goals, pursue our passions, and take risks. We no longer want to waste our limited time on earth, and this newfound drive propels us to live with purpose and intention.

The realization that our time on this planet is limited can be a powerful catalyst for change. It serves as a reminder that life is fleeting and that we have a finite number of opportunities to pursue our dreams and make a positive impact. When we fully grasp the temporary nature of our existence, it ignites a fire within us to seize the day and make every moment count.

Suddenly, the excuses and procrastination that held us back seem trivial in the face of our mortality. We become acutely aware that tomorrow is not guaranteed, and this awareness spurs us into action. We find ourselves taking risks we may have previously avoided, stepping outside our comfort zones, and pursuing the things that truly matter to us.

Embracing our mortality also allows us to let go of the fear of failure. When we recognize that death is an inevitable part of life, we understand that it is better to try and fail than never to try at all. We become more willing to take on challenges, knowing that the real failure lies in not making the attempt. This newfound courage and determination propel us forward, enabling us to achieve things we once thought were beyond our reach.

Acknowledging our mortality can also deepen our connections with others. When we understand that life is fragile and transient, we become more appreciative of our relationships. We prioritize spending quality time with loved ones, expressing our love and gratitude, and resolving conflicts. We recognize the importance of building meaningful connections that transcend the boundaries of time. By embracing our mortality, we create a space for authentic and profound relationships to flourish.

The awareness of our own mortality brings into sharp focus the value of our relationships. We begin to cherish the moments we spend with loved ones and invest our time and energy into nurturing those connections. Petty disagreements and trivial conflicts lose their significance in the face of the bigger picture.

When we confront our mortality, we often gain a deeper appreciation for the people in our lives. We become more attentive listeners, offering our undivided presence during conversations. We learn to set aside distractions and truly engage with others, making them feel seen and heard. This presence and genuine connection strengthen our relationships and create a sense of belonging and support. Try to never talk over someone while they are talking. Offer your undivided attention to people who give you their time.

Moreover, acknowledging our mortality can inspire us to mend broken relationships and bridge the gaps that may have existed in the past. We realize that holding grudges and harboring resentment only hinders our own happiness and the quality of our relationships. We recognize the impermanence of life and the importance of forgiveness and reconciliation.

By embracing our mortality and the transient nature of

existence, we cultivate a sense of gratitude for the people who bring joy and meaning to our lives. We no longer take our relationships for granted but actively work to deepen them, knowing that the time we have with our loved ones is limited.

Confronting our mortality offers a unique vantage point from which we can evaluate the significance of our lives. It allows us to step back from the noise and distractions of everyday existence and reflect on what truly matters. We gain a fresh perspective on our values, beliefs, and aspirations. Trivial concerns fade away, and we focus on what brings us joy, fulfillment, and a sense of purpose. This perspective shift helps us align our actions with our deepest desires, leading to a more fulfilling and meaningful life. We become more discerning about how we spend our time, energy, and resources, investing them in endeavors that bring us genuine satisfaction and a sense of purpose. We let go of the fear of judgment and societal norms, embracing our unique passions and aspirations.

Step 6 Conclusion

In this step, we embarked on a profound exploration of impermanence and mortality, recognizing them as essential aspects of life. We delved into the concept that everything is temporary and the importance of embracing impermanence as a means to unclutter our lives and find deeper meaning and purpose. Furthermore, we confronted the common human tendency to deny death and explored the transformative power of facing our mortality head-on. In the next step, we will explore the interrelated and life-changing concepts of mindfulness, accepting reality, and gratitude for what is.

Step 7. Mindfulness, Accepting Reality, & Gratitude

I n this step, we explore three essential concepts that are closely intertwined and crucial for embracing the philosophy of Swedish Death Cleaning: mindfulness, accepting reality, and gratitude for what is. Swedish Death Cleaning is not just about physically decluttering and organizing our living spaces; it also encourages us to declutter our minds, emotions, and attitudes toward life. By incorporating mindfulness, accepting reality, and practicing gratitude, we can deepen our understanding of the process and find meaning and purpose in the journey of Swedish Death Cleaning.

I. Mindfulness

Mindfulness is a powerful practice that involves bringing our attention to the present moment without judgment or attachment. It requires us to be fully aware of our thoughts, emotions, and sensations as they arise and to observe them without getting caught up in them. By cultivating mindfulness, we can develop a non-reactive and non-judgmental stance toward our experiences, which in turn allows us to gain clarity and insight.

In the context of Swedish Death Cleaning, mindfulness plays a vital role in helping us unclutter our lives and find meaning and purpose. By approaching the process of decluttering and organizing our possessions with a mindful mindset, we can be fully present and engaged in each step. Mindfulness allows us to observe our attachments and emotional reactions to our belongings without being consumed by them. It helps us develop a deeper awareness of our possessions and their significance in our lives. By practicing mindfulness during Swedish Death Cleaning, we can make more intentional decisions about what to keep, discard, or pass on to others.

When we engage in the decluttering process mindfully, we are better able to recognize the emotions that arise as we sort through our possessions. Nostalgia, sadness, and even guilt may surface as we come across items that hold sentimental value or remind us of past experiences. Mindfulness helps us acknowledge these emotions without judgment, allowing us to process them and let go of any negative associations. By mindfully experiencing these emotions, we create space for healing and personal growth.

One way to practice mindfulness during Swedish Death Cleaning is to bring our attention to the physical sensations and feelings that arise as we handle each item. As we touch an object, we can notice its weight, texture, and temperature. We can pay attention to how it feels in our hands and how it affects our posture and movement. By focusing on the physical sensations, we ground ourselves in the present moment and cultivate a deeper connection to our belongings.

Another aspect of mindfulness in Swedish Death Cleaning involves observing our thoughts and mental patterns as we make decisions about what to keep and what to let go of. We can notice any resistance or attachment that arises when considering parting with certain items. We might catch ourselves making justifications or rationalizations for holding onto things that no longer serve us. Mindfulness allows us to recognize these thought patterns without judgment and bring ourselves back to the present moment. It enables us to see the transient nature of our thoughts and emotions, helping us make more informed choices about what truly matters to us.

Practicing mindfulness in Swedish Death Cleaning also means approaching the process with curiosity and open-mindedness. Instead of rushing through the decluttering process to reach an end goal, we can embrace each moment as an opportunity for self-discovery. Mindfulness encourages us to explore the stories and memories associated with our belongings. We can ask ourselves questions like: What role did this item play in my life? How does it make me feel? Does it align with the person I am today? By approaching these questions with a sense of curiosity and open-mindedness, we can uncover deeper insights about ourselves and our values.

Mindfulness isn't just about thoughtfully decluttering our homes and lifestyle. Mindfulness helps us shift our focus from the accumulation of possessions to the appreciation of what we already have, fostering a sense of contentment and fulfillment. Mindfulness influences how we relate to our possessions and our environment on a daily basis. By bringing a mindful awareness to our relationship with material things, we can develop more conscious consumption habits. We become more discerning in our choices, considering the long-term impact of our purchases and whether they truly align with our values. Mindfulness encourages us to cultivate a sense of detachment from material possessions, recognizing that our worth and identity are not defined by what we own.

Things Distract Us From Finding Meaning & Purpose

One significant obstacle on the road to discovering our true meaning and purpose is our attachment to possessions. In today's consumer-driven society, it's easy to accumulate material belongings without considering their impact on our lives. We are often enticed by the latest gadgets, fashion trends, and shiny new objects, but we rarely stop to think about how these possessions affect our overall well-being and our ability to pursue our true passions and goals. The truth is these possessions, while initially appealing, can gradually consume our time, energy, and focus, becoming barriers on our path to finding meaning and purpose.

When we fill our lives with an abundance of material possessions, we create a never-ending cycle of consumption. The more we acquire, the more we desire, and the more time and effort we must invest in maintaining, organizing, and upgrading our belongings. Our possessions begin to take up physical space in our homes, but they also occupy mental and emotional space within us. We find ourselves preoccupied with the pursuit of more, constantly chasing the elusive sense of fulfillment that material goods promise but rarely deliver.

When we declutter, we remove the physical and emotional weight that possessions impose upon us. We liberate ourselves from the constant cycle of acquiring and maintaining things. In doing so, we free up our time, energy, and focus to invest in pursuits that align with our passions and goals. Imagine the hours we spend cleaning and organizing our belongings, searching for misplaced items, or mindlessly scrolling through online shopping websites. Now picture redirecting that energy toward activities that truly ignite our souls – painting, writing, volunteering, starting a business, or spending quality time with loved ones.

The distractions that possessions bring can be deceptive. They trick us into believing that material accumulation equates to success or happiness. We may find ourselves comparing our possessions with those of others, constantly seeking validation through ownership rather than personal growth or meaningful experiences. In reality, these possessions often distract us from the things that truly matter – our relationships, personal development, and the pursuit of our passions. The more time and energy we invest in acquiring and maintaining possessions, the less we have available to invest in ourselves and the things that truly bring us fulfillment.

Letting go of possessions means being intentional about what we bring into our lives and being mindful of how these possessions impact our overall well-being. By consciously choosing to surround ourselves only with the things that truly enhance our lives, we create an environment that supports our journey toward self-discovery, meaning, and purpose.

As we declutter and simplify, we discover a newfound sense of freedom. We no longer feel burdened by the weight of our possessions, or the expectations tied to them. We begin to appreciate the space we have created, both physically and mentally, and the possibilities it holds. Our priorities shift from the pursuit of material accumulation to the pursuit of personal growth, fulfillment, and the pursuit of our passions.

By exploring how possessions can distract us from pursuing our passions and goals, we become aware of the choices we make and the impact they have on our lives. We learn to differentiate between the things that truly bring us joy and those that are merely temporary sources of gratification. With this awareness, we can intentionally curate our environment, surrounding ourselves with objects and experiences that align with our values and aspirations.

Things Have Nothing to Do with Our Value & Identity

When we tie our sense of self solely to the things we own, we limit our potential for growth, fulfillment, and meaningful connections. Liberating ourselves from this narrow perspective allows us to delve deeper into the essence of who we are and discover the authentic sources of meaning and purpose in our lives.

Our identity is an intricate tapestry skillfully woven from diverse threads. Possessions may provide glimpses into our external preferences, yet they are mere reflections of our true selves. To truly understand our identity, we must delve into our beliefs, passions, relationships, and experiences.

One crucial component of identity lies within our beliefs. Our deeply held convictions about the world, ourselves, and others shape our perspectives and guide our actions. Whether rooted in faith, philosophy, or personal values, our beliefs give rise to the principles by which we navigate life. Through these beliefs, we find our moral compass, illuminating the path to meaning and purpose.

Passions also play a vital role in shaping our identity. The things that ignite our enthusiasm, stir our souls, and drive us to action reflect aspects of our true selves. Whether it be a love for art, nature, music, or science, our passions infuse our lives with vitality and bring us closer to our authentic essence. Engaging with these passions connects us to our core identity and fills our existence with a profound sense of purpose.

Furthermore, our relationships contribute significantly to the tapestry of our identity. The connections we forge with family, friends, and communities provide fertile ground for personal growth and self-discovery. Through the lens of our interactions with others, we gain insights into our strengths, weaknesses, and areas for improvement. The bonds we nurture with those we care about offer us support, affirmation, and a mirror in which we can see our own character reflected.

Experiences, too, shape the mosaic of our identity. Life is an ever-unfolding journey, and each encounter, triumph, setback, and adventure leave an indelible mark on who we are. Through adversity, we discover resilience and inner strength. Through joy, we find moments of pure, unfiltered happiness. It is the collection of these experiences, woven together, that give depth and texture to our sense of self.

Our identity flourishes when we cultivate and express our inner qualities. The virtues we embody—kindness, compassion, integrity, humility—reside within us, independent of material possessions. These qualities define our character and determine the impact we have on the world. They transcend the superficial and form the foundation of our relationships, the seeds of change we sow, and the legacy we leave behind.

When we detach our identity from possessions, we liberate ourselves from the constraints of societal expectations and consumerist culture. We become free to explore the dimensions of our being that truly matter—those that contribute to our personal growth, happiness, and fulfillment. We embark on a journey of self-discovery, peeling away the layers of external validation to unearth the treasures within.

Living fully in the present moment is an integral part of this process. When we immerse ourselves in the richness of the present, we cultivate a profound sense of presence and awareness. By shifting our focus from accumulating possessions to embracing experiences, we enrich our lives immeasurably.

Our true identity is not found in possessions but in the intangible aspects of our existence. It resides in our beliefs, passions, relationships, experiences, and the virtues we embody. By disentangling ourselves from the notion that our worth is determined by what we own, we open ourselves up to a world of infinite possibilities. We can embark on a journey of self-discovery, embracing our authentic selves and living fully in the present. In this pursuit, we find meaning, purpose, and a profound understanding of who we are and what truly matters.

Strategies for Mindfully Cultivating Our True Identity

This section explores various practices and mindset shifts that can help us find a deeper sense of our value, meaning, and purpose within ourselves. By focusing on internal factors and embracing non-material aspects of life, we can break free from the cycle of materialism and discover a more meaningful and fulfilling existence.

Practice Self-Reflection

One of the foundational steps in cultivating self-esteem independent of possessions is to embark on a journey of self-reflection. Take the time to delve into your values, strengths, and passions. What truly brings you joy and a sense of fulfillment? Reflect on your accomplishments and personal growth, acknowledging the internal factors that have contributed to your success rather than solely relying on external achievements. By gaining clarity on your authentic self, you can begin to cultivate a stronger sense of self-worth that goes beyond the accumulation of possessions.

Develop Self-Compassion

In a society that often equates self-worth with external achievements, it's crucial to practice self-compassion. Treat yourself with kindness and understanding, acknowledging that your worth as an individual is not defined by possessions. Engage in self-care activities that nourish your mind, body, and soul.

Take time to rest, engage in hobbies you enjoy, and surround yourself with positive influences. Cultivating self-compassion involves embracing your imperfections, learning from your mistakes, and celebrating your strengths. By developing a genuine sense of self-acceptance, you can build a foundation of self-esteem that remains resilient even in the absence of material possessions.

Discover & Pursue Hobbies that Align with Your Values & Interests

Volunteer your time and skills to help others or engage in creative endeavors that allow you to express yourself authentically. By focusing on activities that nourish your soul and contribute to your personal growth, you'll find a deep sense of fulfillment that transcends the temporary satisfaction of material possessions.

Surround Yourself with Supportive Relationships

The people we surround ourselves with have a profound impact on our self-esteem and overall well-being. Cultivate relationships with individuals who value you for who you are rather than what you possess. Seek out connections that nurture personal growth, inspire self-acceptance, and encourage you to embrace your intrinsic worth. Surrounding yourself with a supportive community helps reinforce the belief in your inherent value beyond material possessions. These relationships provide a safe space where you can authentically express yourself and cultivate a sense of belonging that is not contingent on what you own.

Cultivating Mindfulness in the Present Moment

Mindfulness, a powerful tool for loving and accepting reality, involves intentionally bringing our attention to the present moment without judgment. It is a practice that allows us to fully engage with our surroundings, experiences, and emotions. By cultivating mindfulness, we develop the ability to appreciate the beauty and richness of each moment, no matter how ordinary or extraordinary it may seem. Through mindfulness, we can truly live fully and find profound meaning and purpose in our lives.

In our fast-paced and hectic world, it is all too easy to get caught up in the endless stream of thoughts and distractions that pull us away from the present moment. We are constantly bombarded with notifications, responsibilities, and worries about the future or regrets about the past. Our minds often wander, lost in a sea of thoughts, and we become disconnected from the richness and depth of our immediate experience.

Practicing mindfulness offers us an antidote to this modern predicament. It invites us to pause, to slow down, and to direct our attention to the here and now. Through mindfulness, we become more attuned to the subtleties of life—the sound of birds chirping outside our window, the warmth of the morning sun on our faces, or the taste of a freshly brewed cup of coffee. We begin to notice the intricate details and nuances that surround us, which we might have otherwise overlooked.

Mindfulness teaches us to savor and appreciate the simple pleasures that often go unnoticed in our busy lives. We learn to drink deeply from the well of each moment, fully immersing ourselves in the present experience. Whether it is the vibrant colors of a sunset or the warmth of the sun on our skin, mindfulness allows us to fully participate in these moments and extract their essence.

When we cultivate mindfulness, we create a spaciousness that allows us to observe our thoughts, emotions, and sensations as they arise. This self-awareness becomes the foundation for accepting and embracing reality with a compassionate heart. We recognize that the present moment is the only place where life truly unfolds. It is the canvas upon which our experiences are painted, the stage upon which our stories are enacted.

By anchoring ourselves firmly in the present, we can let go of the burdens of the past and the anxieties of the future. We release the grip of worries and regrets that weigh us down, and instead, we embrace the beauty and potential that lie within each passing moment. Mindfulness offers us a refuge from the relentless pull of time, inviting us to experience life in its fullness, unencumbered by the constraints of the past or future.

Practicing mindfulness is not about escaping or denying the challenges and difficulties of life. Instead, it is about meeting them with open-hearted awareness and acceptance. Mindfulness allows us to hold our joys and sorrows, our successes and failures, in a compassionate embrace. It teaches us that all experiences, whether pleasant or unpleasant, are an integral part of the tapestry of our existence.

As we cultivate mindfulness, we begin to recognize the impermanence of all things. We understand that life is a series of fleeting moments, each one unique and irreplaceable. This awareness infuses our lives with a sense of urgency to fully live, to love deeply, and to engage wholeheartedly with the world around us. We no longer postpone our happiness or postpone our dreams. Instead, we make the choice to live fully now, in this very moment.

In the stillness of mindfulness, we discover an inner wellspring of peace and contentment that transcends the ups and downs of external circumstances. We learn to tap into a deep well of wisdom and insight that resides within us all. By cultivating mindfulness, we become active participants in our lives rather than passive spectators. We reclaim our power to shape our own destiny and to create a life that is aligned with our true values and aspirations.

Cultivating mindfulness is a lifelong journey, a practice that requires commitment, patience, and self-compassion. It is not a destination to be reached but rather a path to be walked with intention and curiosity. As we deepen our practice, we discover that mindfulness is not confined to formal meditation sessions. It can be infused into every aspect of our lives—while we eat, walk, work, or interact with others.

Mindfulness is a gateway to living fully and finding profound meaning and purpose in our lives. It allows us to appreciate the present moment, savor simple pleasures, and cultivate a deep sense of gratitude and interconnectedness. By anchoring ourselves firmly in the present, we can let go of the burdens of the past and the anxieties of the future. Mindfulness invites us to live fully now, to love deeply, and to engage wholeheartedly with the world around us. Through mindfulness, we awaken to the inherent wisdom and beauty that reside within us and within each passing moment.

One of the keys to finding joy in everyday experiences is to approach each day with a sense of curiosity and wonder. Cultivate a childlike mindset that embraces novelty and seeks out the extraordinary within the ordinary. Challenge yourself to notice the small miracles that unfold around you—a blooming flower, a kind gesture from a stranger, or a moment of unexpected beauty. When we open ourselves up to these experiences, we allow ourselves to be fully alive and engaged with the world.

Additionally, finding joy in the simple things is not just about our own personal fulfillment; it also has a ripple effect on those around us. When we radiate gratitude and joy, we inspire others to do the same. By sharing our appreciation for life's small treasures, we create a positive and uplifting environment that fosters deeper connections and a greater sense of community.

The path to living a meaningful and purposeful life lies in finding joy and gratitude in the simple things and everyday experiences. By shifting our focus to the present, cultivating mindfulness, and embracing a mindset of gratitude, we unlock a world of beauty and fulfillment. Let us not overlook the laughter of a loved one, the aroma of a home-cooked meal, or the feeling of grass beneath our feet. Instead, let us approach each moment with open hearts and open minds, savoring the richness of life and finding true meaning in the seemingly insignificant moments.

Letting Go of Attachment to Desired Outcomes

One of the key obstacles we face in loving and accepting reality is our attachment to specific outcomes. We tend to have preconceived notions of how things should be or how our lives should unfold. We create mental images of the perfect job, the ideal relationship, or the successful accomplishment of our goals. We invest so much of our energy and emotional well-being in these desired outcomes that when reality doesn't align with our expectations, we are left feeling frustrated, disappointed, or even despairing.

To truly embrace reality and find meaning and purpose in our lives, it is essential to learn the art of letting go of attachment to desired outcomes. This does not imply giving up on our goals or dreams; rather, it involves releasing our grip on how things "should" be and opening ourselves to the infinite possibilities of the present moment. By relinquishing our attachment, we create space for new opportunities and unexpected blessings to enter our lives.

Letting go of attachment is a profound shift in mindset—a shift that requires us to adopt a perspective of trust and surrender. It entails recognizing that life's unfolding is often beyond our control and that there is wisdom and beauty in embracing the unknown. When we release our expectations and wholeheartedly embrace the present moment as it is, we free ourselves from the burden of disappointment and create room for authentic growth and transformation.

At first, the idea of letting go of attachment may seem daunting. We may fear that by relinquishing our desires, we are surrendering our ambitions and settling for less. However, the practice of non-attachment does not mean becoming passive or apathetic. It is about developing a sense of inner peace and contentment that is not dependent on external circumstances. It is about recognizing that true fulfillment and happiness come from within rather than from the attainment of specific outcomes.

When we become fixated on a particular outcome, we close ourselves off to other possibilities that may be equally or even more fulfilling. By letting go of attachment to specific outcomes, we open ourselves to the serendipitous, mysterious, and unexpected paths that life may present to us. We learn to trust that the universe has a way of orchestrating events for our highest good, even if they may not align with our initial expectations.

In the process of letting go of attachment, we may encounter resistance and discomfort. Our attachment to desired outcomes is often rooted in deeply ingrained beliefs and fears. We may fear failure, rejection, or the unknown. It is important to approach this process with self-compassion and patience. Be gentle with yourself as you navigate the terrain of releasing attachments and remember that it is a journey that unfolds gradually.

As we let go of attachment to desired outcomes, we begin to experience a sense of liberation and freedom. We no longer feel bound by rigid expectations or imprisoned by the fear of disappointment. Instead, we open ourselves to the vast array of possibilities that exist in every moment. We discover that meaning and purpose are not found in the destination but in the journey itself.

By embracing the present moment, trusting in the wisdom of how life is unfolding, and letting go of attachment, we create the space for profound transformation and growth. We become more attuned to the subtle nuances of life and more receptive to the lessons that each experience offers. We find joy and fulfillment in the simple pleasures and unexpected blessings that arise along the way. Ultimately, by living fully in the present moment, unburdened by attachment to desired outcomes, we discover a deeper connection to ourselves, to others, and to the world around us. We find meaning and purpose in the very act of being alive.

Embracing Life's Imperfections & Finding Beauty in Them

In a world that often promotes perfectionism and the relentless pursuit of flawlessness, it can be challenging to embrace imperfections. However, loving and accepting reality requires us to recognize and appreciate the beauty that exists within imperfection. Every aspect of life has its flaws, including ourselves. Rather than viewing these imperfections as shortcomings, we can shift our perspective and see them as unique characteristics that contribute to our individuality and humanity. Embracing imperfections allows us to embrace ourselves and others with compassion and understanding.

When we look around, we see a world that strives for flawlessness in various aspects. From the airbrushed images in magazines to carefully curated social media feeds, society constantly bombards us with an unattainable standard of perfection. We are led to believe that only the flawless and faultless can be considered beautiful or successful. This pressure to conform to an idealized version of ourselves often leaves us feeling inadequate and discontented.

However, the truth is that imperfections are an inherent part of the human experience. They are what make us unique and authentic. Rather than seeking to hide or eradicate our imperfections, we should embrace them as an integral part of who we are. By doing so, we not only cultivate self-acceptance but also create an environment of acceptance and understanding for others.

Embracing imperfections, whether they are your own, someone else's, or imperfections in life itself, begins with a shift in perspective. Instead of viewing our flaws as shortcomings, we can choose to perceive them as unique qualities that contribute to our individuality. Take, for instance, the beauty of a cherished antique piece of furniture adorned with worn edges and subtle blemishes. These imperfections narrate its journey and add character to its overall appearance. Similarly, our own imperfections carry tales of resilience, growth, and the lessons we have learned along the way. They are the marks of our experiences and the proof of a life fully lived.

When we embrace our imperfections, we unlock the door to self-compassion. We cease to criticize ourselves for our mistakes or limitations; instead, we embrace kindness and understanding. This self-compassion empowers us to navigate life with curiosity and openness, recognizing that our imperfections do not define us but rather foster personal growth. By accepting the imperfections of others, we communicate love and acceptance. And when we embrace the world as God wants it, we demonstrate our unwavering trust and love for the divine.

Moreover, imperfections can teach us valuable lessons and offer opportunities for growth. When we approach challenges with an open heart and a willingness to learn, we discover that even the most difficult circumstances can become catalysts for personal transformation and profound wisdom. In the face of adversity, our imperfections become the very tools we need to navigate the complexities of life.

For example, let's consider a person who has struggled with social anxiety for most of their life. Initially, they may view this imperfection as a hindrance, preventing them from fully engaging with others and pursuing their dreams. However, when they choose to embrace their social anxiety and see it as a unique aspect of their personality, they can begin to explore ways to manage it and find new avenues for personal growth. Through this process, they may develop deep empathy and understanding for others facing similar challenges, leading them to pursue a career in counseling or advocacy. In this way, what was once seen as an imperfection becomes a source of strength and purpose.

Embracing imperfections also allows us to cultivate resilience. Life is full of setbacks and failures, and our imperfections can serve as reminders that it's okay to stumble and make mistakes. By accepting that imperfection is an inevitable part of the journey, we become better equipped to bounce back from adversity and persevere in the face of challenges. We learn to see failures not as signs of inadequacy but as steppingstones toward growth and self-improvement.

Furthermore, embracing imperfections in ourselves helps us develop empathy and compassion for others. When we recognize our own flaws and struggles, we are more likely to extend understanding and forgiveness to those around us. Instead of judging others for their imperfections, we can approach them with empathy, recognizing that we are all on a similar journey of self-discovery and growth.

In our pursuit of perfection, we often overlook the beauty that exists within imperfections. Just as a mosaic is created from broken pieces, our lives are made whole and meaningful by integrating what we perceive as our strengths and imperfections. Embracing imperfections allows us to celebrate the full spectrum of the human experience, with all its complexities, vulnerabilities, and triumphs.

Embracing imperfections is a powerful act of self-love and acceptance. By shifting our perspective and seeing imperfections as unique characteristics that contribute to our individuality, we open ourselves up to self-compassion, personal growth, and profound wisdom. Imperfections are not flaws to be hidden or fixed but rather opportunities for self-discovery, resilience, and connection with others. In a world that often emphasizes perfection, embracing imperfections is a courageous and transformative choice that leads us to find true meaning and purpose in our lives.

By embracing the concept of gratitude and accepting reality as it unfolds in the present moment, we embark on a transformative journey that liberates us from the shackles of resistance and denial. In doing so, we open ourselves to a world brimming with beauty, hidden opportunities, and profound experiences that are often concealed within the fabric of the ordinary.

Through the Swedish Death Cleaning process, which emphasizes decluttering and simplifying our lives, a profound shift in perspective occurs. As we let go of the physical and emotional baggage that weighs us down, we create space for gratitude and contentment to flourish. By relinquishing attachment to material possessions and embracing the imperfections inherent in our lives, we pave the way for a deeper appreciation of the present moment.

Practicing mindfulness and cultivating conscious awareness become instrumental in our journey toward finding meaning and purpose. Mindfulness, often described as the art of paying attention to the present moment without judgment, enables us to fully immerse ourselves in the richness of our experiences. It allows us to savor the intricate details that might have otherwise gone unnoticed, and it invites us to engage with life on a profound level.

When we live fully in the present, we no longer allow ourselves to be consumed by regrets of the past or anxieties about the future. Instead, we direct our attention to what is happening right now, understanding that it is the only moment we truly have control over. By embracing the transitory nature of life and recognizing the impermanence of all things, we learn to cherish each passing moment as a precious gift.

Within the context of Swedish Death Cleaning, the practice of living fully in the present takes on added significance. As we navigate the process of decluttering and organizing our physical environment, we are invited to engage with our possessions and memories consciously. Instead of mindlessly discarding or holding onto items out of habit or fear, we develop a heightened sense of discernment.

We learn to recognize the objects that truly hold meaning and significance in our lives and those that no longer serve a purpose. We acknowledge that sentimental value resides not merely in the physical presence of an item but in the memories and emotions it evokes. By choosing to let go of certain possessions, we create space for new relationships, experiences, and opportunities to enter our lives.

Moreover, living fully in the present grants us the clarity to discern what truly matters to us. As we gain a deeper understanding of our values, passions, and aspirations, we become empowered to align our actions with our authentic selves. We no longer chase after fleeting desires or succumb to societal pressures that distract us from our true path.

Gratitude, which we will explore more deeply at the end of this chapter, becomes a way of life—a lens through which we view the world. It reminds us to pause and acknowledge the blessings that often go unnoticed amidst the chaos of daily life. By cultivating gratitude, we shift our focus from what is lacking to what is abundant, from what is broken to what is whole. In doing so, we nurture a deep sense of contentment that transcends the pursuit of external validation or material wealth.

The wisdom of Swedish Death Cleaning lies not merely in its practicality but in its profound invitation to embrace the present moment. Through the practice of gratitude and acceptance, we unlock the true essence of a meaningful life. We learn that meaning and purpose are not elusive destinations to be reached but rather states of being that can be accessed in each passing moment.

By learning to love and accept reality as it is in the present moment, we embark on a transformative journey that invites us to live fully. The wisdom of Swedish Death Cleaning teaches us to embrace imperfections, release attachment, and cultivate gratitude. Through mindfulness and conscious awareness, we immerse ourselves in the richness of each passing moment, uncovering the true essence of a meaningful life. Let us embrace this wisdom and embark on a life-affirming path of gratitude and purpose.

Mindfulness to Find Meaning & Purpose

In modern life, it is easy to lose sight of what truly matters. We get caught up in the never-ending pursuit of material possessions, accomplishments, and societal expectations, often neglecting our own well-being and the deeper questions of life. However, by cultivating mindfulness, we can unlock the power to find meaning and purpose amidst the chaos.

Mindfulness, at its core, is the practice of being fully present in the moment, aware of our thoughts, feelings, bodily sensations, and the world around us. It is a state of non-judgmental awareness that allows us to embrace each experience with curiosity and acceptance. When we engage in mindfulness, we step out of autopilot mode and into a space where we can connect with ourselves and the world in a more meaningful way.

Finding meaning and purpose is a deeply personal and subjective journey. It involves reflecting on our values, passions, and the things that bring us joy and fulfillment. Mindfulness serves as a compass in this journey, helping us navigate through the noise and distractions to discover what truly resonates with our authentic selves.

Through mindfulness, we can cultivate a heightened sense of self-awareness. We become attuned to our thoughts, emotions, and bodily sensations, noticing the patterns and habits that shape our lives. By observing these patterns without judgment, we gain insights into our deepest desires and motivations. This self-awareness allows us to align our actions and choices with our values and aspirations, leading us toward a more purposeful life.

Furthermore, mindfulness helps us cultivate gratitude for what is. In a culture that constantly emphasizes what we lack or need to achieve, it is easy to lose sight of the abundance that already exists in our lives. Mindfulness allows us to shift our focus toward gratitude, acknowledging and appreciating the blessings, big and small, that surround us. This gratitude cultivates contentment and a sense of fulfillment, reminding us that we have enough and that we are enough.

Meaning and purpose are closely intertwined with self-actualization—the process of becoming the best version of ourselves and realizing our full potential. Mindfulness serves as a powerful tool for self-actualization by providing a platform for self-reflection, growth, and transformation. As we become more mindful, we gain clarity about our strengths, weaknesses, and the areas where we can grow. We become more attuned to our passions and interests, empowering us to pursue endeavors that align with our true calling.

Ultimately, mindfulness is a lifelong practice that requires commitment, patience, and a willingness to explore the depths of our own being. As we embark on this journey of self-discovery, we find meaning and purpose not in the external trappings of success but in the richness of our inner world and the connections we foster with others.

The wisdom of Swedish Death Cleaning encourages us to unclutter our lives physically, mentally, and emotionally. Through the practice of mindfulness, we can declutter our minds and strip away the unnecessary distractions that cloud our vision. By embracing the present moment, cultivating gratitude, and nurturing our own growth, we unlock the door to a life filled with meaning, purpose, and self-actualization.

II. Accepting Reality

On the path to discovering meaning and purpose, acknowledging and embracing reality in the present moment is crucial to finding fulfillment and living authentically. Often, we find ourselves resisting or denying the truth of our circumstances, clinging to past regrets, or fixating on future aspirations. However, the practice of loving and accepting reality requires us to release these tendencies and open ourselves to the truth of the present.

The first step toward transformation is recognizing our natural inclination to resist or deny reality. As humans, we often romanticize the past or idealize the future. We may long for a different past, dwell on what could have been, or daydream about a seemingly better future. While it is natural to reflect on the past or plan for the future, it becomes problematic when we resist accepting the reality of the present. By acknowledging this tendency within us, we can consciously choose to shift our perspective and embrace the truth of the present.

Resisting or denying reality often stems from a fear of the unknown. We may fear change, feel uncertain about life's outcomes, or be unwilling to confront difficult emotions. In our pursuit of meaning and purpose, it is essential to recognize that growth and fulfillment come from embracing the reality of our current circumstances, no matter how challenging or uncomfortable they may be.

One common form of resistance is holding onto past regrets.

We may replay mistakes or missed opportunities in our minds, tormenting ourselves with thoughts of what could have been. However, dwelling on the past only perpetuates feelings of guilt, shame, and dissatisfaction. It prevents us from fully engaging with the present and discovering the meaning and purpose it holds. Instead of getting caught in a cycle of regret, we can choose to learn from our past experiences, extract wisdom from them, and apply it to our present moment.

Similarly, fixating on an idealized future can hinder our ability to live fully in the present. We may believe that our happiness and fulfillment lie in achieving specific goals or acquiring particular possessions. While it is important to set goals and work toward them, pinning all our hopes on the future blinds us to the richness of the present. By constantly yearning for something beyond our reach, we miss out on the beauty and opportunities that surround us right now. Striking a balance between striving for future aspirations and savoring the present moment is vital.

When we resist or deny reality, we disconnect from the truth of our experiences. We create narratives that shield us from uncomfortable truths, distorting our perception of ourselves and the world around us. This disconnection prevents us from fully engaging with life and hampers our ability to find meaning and purpose.

However, by choosing to embrace reality and live in the present moment, we open ourselves up to profound growth and transformation. Accepting the truth of our circumstances allows us to engage fully with the present moment, responding authentically and consciously. It empowers us to make choices aligned with our values and aspirations, bringing us closer to a life of purpose and fulfillment.

To cultivate the practice of embracing reality, we can incorporate various techniques into our daily lives. Mindfulness meditation, for instance, helps us develop awareness of our thoughts and emotions without judgment. By observing our mental and emotional patterns, we can identify moments of resistance or denial and consciously choose to let them go. Mindfulness allows us to anchor ourselves in the present moment, cultivating a deep acceptance of what is and reducing the impulse to escape into what should be.

Furthermore, surrounding ourselves with a supportive community greatly aids us on this journey. Connecting with like-minded individuals who share our values and aspirations provides encouragement, accountability, and different perspectives. Engaging in meaningful conversations and sharing our struggles and triumphs with others fosters a sense of belonging and reminds us that we are not alone in our quest for meaning and purpose. Through collective wisdom and shared experiences, we gain insights that help us navigate the challenges of accepting reality and inspire us to live authentically.

Recognizing our tendency to resist or deny reality is a crucial step toward living fully and finding meaning and purpose. By acknowledging this inclination within us, we can consciously choose to embrace the truth of the present moment. Letting go of past regrets and releasing the fixation on an idealized future allows us to engage with our current circumstances authentically. By embracing reality, we open ourselves to growth, transformation, and the discovery of a deeply meaningful and purposeful life.

Through practices such as mindfulness, gratitude, and community connection, we can cultivate the ability to live fully in the present and unlock the wisdom that resides within us. These practices enable us to embrace the reality of what is rather than getting stuck in what should be. They empower us to navigate life's uncertainties with grace and resilience, honoring our authentic selves and finding fulfillment in the present moment. By accepting reality and embracing the truth of our experiences, we embark on a transformative journey toward a life of meaning, purpose, and deep fulfillment.

III. Gratitude for What Is

We must learn to be grateful for life as it is rather than how we believe it should be. A significant portion of our mental clutter arises from our judgmental perspective that life is somehow flawed and things aren't unfolding as we had planned. When we cultivate gratitude for life as it is, our stress, anxiety, and mental turmoil can diminish. The more time we spend in our heads arguing with life about what is, the more suffering we will experience. Whenever we argue with reality—what is happening in the here and now—we always experience pain and suffering.

We must also accept ourselves, strengths and weaknesses, be grateful for who we are, and not spend our lives focusing on who we think we should be. There's nothing wrong with self-improvement, but true happiness and gratitude stem from accepting our authentic selves in the present moment. Only by embracing our authentic selves with gratitude in the present moment can we begin to accept and be grateful for the individuals and circumstances that enter into our lives.

Gratitude for what is entails cultivating a sense of appreciation and thankfulness for the present moment and the things we already have in our lives. It involves recognizing the value and significance of our possessions, relationships, and experiences and acknowledging the positive impact they have on our well-being. Gratitude allows us to shift our focus from what we lack to what we already possess, promoting contentment and a sense of abundance.

The mindfulness of Swedish Death Cleaning invites us to practice gratitude throughout our daily lives. When we approach decluttering with gratitude, we shift our mindset from a scarcity mentality to an abundance mindset. We become aware of the value and usefulness of the items we own, and we express gratitude for the role they have played in our lives. Gratitude helps us let go of the guilt associated with discarding or giving away certain possessions, as we recognize that they have served their purpose and can now bring joy to someone else's life.

Moreover, practicing gratitude during Swedish Death Cleaning allows us to appreciate the memories and experiences associated with our belongings. It helps us acknowledge the impact that certain objects have had on our personal journeys, even if they no longer serve a practical purpose. By expressing gratitude for these items, we honor the past and create a positive narrative around letting go.

Gratitude is a transformative force that has the power to shift our perspective and elevate our well-being. It is the art of acknowledging and appreciating the blessings, big and small, that grace our lives each day. When we open our hearts to gratitude, we awaken to the richness and depth of the present moment. We become attuned to the intricacies of life and start to notice the simple joys that often go unnoticed.

To fully embrace gratitude and accept reality in the present moment, we must first let go of the attachments and preoccupations that bind us to the past or future. The Swedish Death Cleaning philosophy encourages us to release the clutter of physical possessions, but it can also extend to decluttering our minds and emotions. By clearing our mental and emotional space, we create room for gratitude to flourish.

One powerful practice that can deepen our gratitude is keeping a gratitude journal. Each day, take a few moments to reflect on and write down three things you are grateful for. They can be as simple as the smell of a flower, the wind blowing through your hair or the taste of a delicious meal. By consistently practicing gratitude, we train our minds to focus on the positive aspects of our lives, fostering a sense of contentment and appreciation.

Even in the face of death, the concept of gratitude is a powerful tool that can help us unlock the door to the present moment. By developing an attitude of gratitude, we shift our focus from what is lacking in our lives to what is already abundant. Gratitude allows us to recognize and appreciate the blessings and opportunities that surround us each day, no matter how big or small they may seem.

Gratitude for the Present Moment

Through mindfulness, we cultivate a deep sense of gratitude for the present moment. We realize that each breath is a gift, each step a miracle. We learn to appreciate the interconnectedness of all people and all things and the profound interplay between ourselves and the world around us. Mindfulness enables us to see the extraordinary within the ordinary and to find meaning and purpose in the simplest of acts.

When we cultivate gratitude for what is, we acknowledge that life is a series of experiences, and each moment carries its own unique value. It is not always easy to accept reality as it is, especially when faced with difficulties, challenges, or disappointments. However, by learning to accept and embrace what is, we free ourselves from the burden of resistance and open ourselves up to the endless possibilities that exist in the here and now.

Regrets and anxieties often weigh heavily on our minds. Similarly, worries and expectations can cast a shadow over our lives, preventing us from fully immersing ourselves in the present moment. Mindfulness and gratitude teach us to acknowledge these worries and expectations, recognize their transient nature, and let go of the grip they have on us. By doing so, we create serenity and peace in our inner space.

The mindfulness of Swedish Death Cleaning invites us to embrace the paradox of life and death, acknowledge the impermanence of all things, and find beauty in the temporary nature of existence. It teaches us that by accepting reality as it is, by letting go of regrets and anxieties, and by embracing the present moment with gratitude, we can live more authentically and fully.

Accepting reality does not mean resigning ourselves to a passive existence or giving up on our dreams and aspirations. On the contrary, it is about acknowledging and working with the circumstances we find ourselves in. When we accept reality, we let go of the need for things to be different, and we focus our energy on taking meaningful action in the present moment.

When we learn to live fully in the present moment, we discover a deep sense of peace, fulfillment, and purpose. We become more attuned to our authentic selves, our passions, and the values that truly matter to us. We cultivate richer and more meaningful relationships as we connect with others from a place of genuine presence and gratitude. We find inspiration and joy in the simplest of things, and our lives become infused with a sense of wonder and awe.

Gratitude shifts our focus from what is lacking to what is abundant and positive in our lives. By practicing gratitude, we cultivate a mindset of appreciation and open ourselves up to the possibilities and opportunities surrounding us. Gratitude helps us recognize the beauty in the ordinary, the blessings in the mundane, and the lessons in life's hardships. Gratitude fosters a sense of contentment and fulfillment, reminding us of the richness of our lives beyond material possessions or external achievements.

Living a Purposeful Life Infused with Gratitude

Living a purposeful life infused with gratitude requires a deliberate and mindful approach to shaping our priorities, establishing meaningful goals, and embracing intentionality in our everyday actions. It involves aligning our values, passions, and aspirations to make intentional choices that contribute to our personal growth and fulfillment.

Gratitude is the foundation of our purpose-driven life. It begins with recognizing and acknowledging the blessings and meaningful aspects of our existence. By cultivating gratitude, we develop a profound appreciation for what we have, fostering contentment and joy in the present moment. Instead of always yearning for more, we learn to find fulfillment in what we already possess and experience. Gratitude allows us to see the beauty and abundance that surrounds us, even in the midst of life's challenges.

Living with meaning and purpose means finding the balance between chasing our dreams and cherishing the blessings we already have. By expressing gratitude for our current circumstances, we create a positive mindset that attracts even more abundance into our lives. When we focus on what we are grateful for, we gain a clearer perspective on our true priorities, helping us make intentional choices aligned with our values and passions.

To live a purposeful life, we must start by determining our priorities with gratitude in mind. Instead of merely considering what we desire, we reflect on what we are thankful for and how these blessings align with our deepest values. Gratitude becomes a guiding force in setting our goals and directing our efforts, allowing us to allocate our time, energy, and resources toward endeavors that matter the most, ensuring a purposeful journey that brings genuine satisfaction.

When we establish our priorities based on gratitude, our goals take on a new dimension. We set SMART goals with an appreciation for the opportunities that lie ahead and the progress we will make. SMART goals are specific, measurable, achievable, relevant, and time bound. This mindful approach ensures that our aspirations are not driven solely by external pressures or comparisons with others but by a sincere desire to grow and contribute positively to the world around us.

Living with intention and gratitude also involves finding balance in all aspects of our lives. We acknowledge that our well-being is multifaceted and that nurturing our physical, emotional, and spiritual health is crucial to leading a purposeful life. By taking care of ourselves holistically, we ensure that we are better equipped to pursue our goals and make meaningful contributions to the world.

Incorporating gratitude into our daily lives enriches our relationships and connections with others. We express appreciation for the people who support and inspire us, creating a positive and nurturing environment that fosters growth and collaboration. Gratitude strengthens our bonds and encourages us to uplift one another, magnifying the impact we can make collectively.

Living with gratitude and purpose unlocks the full potential of our lives. By reflecting on our values, passions, and blessings, we can identify our true priorities and make intentional choices that align with them. Setting SMART goals with gratitude as our compass provides us with direction and purpose, ensuring our efforts are focused and meaningful.

Embracing mindfulness and accepting reality with an open heart allows us to navigate life's challenges with grace and find contentment along the way. By embracing these principles, we can live each day with clarity, purpose, and profound gratitude, uncluttering our lives to discover the true richness and fulfillment that lie within us.

Step 7 Conclusion

Mindfulness, accepting reality, and gratitude for what is are integral concepts in the philosophy of Swedish Death Cleaning. These three concepts intertwine and reinforce each other, providing a framework for decluttering not just our physical spaces but also our minds and attitudes toward life. By cultivating mindfulness, accepting reality as it is, and practicing gratitude, we can live our lives with a deeper understanding, finding meaning and purpose in the process. These concepts encourage us to live in the present, cherish what truly matters, and create space for a more intentional and fulfilling life.

Conclusion

As we reach the end of this transformative journey, let us reflect on the profound changes that have taken place within our hearts and minds. From the moment we embarked on the path of Swedish Death Cleaning, our lives have been touched by a powerful force—a force that has led us to unclutter not only our external world but also the depths of our inner souls.

We have emerged as individuals who are more connected to our true selves, living with purpose, intention, and a newfound appreciation for the present moment.

Step 1: The Art of Swedish Death Cleaning: Keep, Donate, Sell,

Recycle, or Trash

The first step of Swedish Death Cleaning introduced us to the practical aspects of decluttering our living spaces. We learned to make conscious decisions about our possessions holding each item in our hands and asking ourselves if it truly brought us joy or served a purpose. In letting go of the unnecessary, we created physical space that allowed for clarity and freedom. But it was not just about the material objects; it was about the mindset we cultivated—the ability to discern what truly matters in our lives and what can be released.

Step 2: Share Your Legacy with Loved Ones

As we dove deeper into our journey, we discovered the importance of sharing our stories, experiences, and wisdom with our loved ones. We realized that our true legacy was not found in the accumulation of our possessions, but in the impact we have on the lives of others. By opening up and sharing our journey, we created a bridge between generations, nurturing connections that will endure beyond our time on this earth. In doing so, we forged a legacy of love, compassion, and understanding—a legacy that transcends the boundaries of material possessions.

Step 3: Digitize Old Photos, Documents & Memorabilia

In the digital age, we are fortunate to have the tools to preserve our memories in a more accessible and lasting form. Through the process of digitizing our old photos, documents, and memorabilia, we not only freed up physical space but also ensured that our cherished memories would be preserved for future generations. The act of carefully curating and organizing these digital archives became an opportunity for reflection and gratitude an acknowledgment of the richness and beauty of our lives.

Step 4: Leave an Uncluttered Legacy: Finances, Will, & Funeral Plans

Acknowledging the impermanence of life, we turned our attention to the practical matters that often go unaddressed until it is too late. By taking control of our finances, drafting our wills, and making funeral plans, we eased the burden on our loved ones during a time of grief. In doing so, we demonstrated our love and consideration for them, providing a clear path forward and allowing them the space to mourn and remember us without the weight of practical concerns. Our uncluttered legacy will be our final act of care and love.

Step 5: The Power of Simplicity and Minimalism

As we embraced simplicity and minimalism, we realized that

these principles extended far beyond the physical realm. They penetrated the depths of our souls, guiding us to shed the layers of complexity that had accumulated over the years. In the process, we discovered the freedom and clarity that comes from letting go of the unnecessary—both externally and internally. Simplicity became a guiding force, leading us to a life that is aligned with our values, passions, and true desires.

Step 6: Everything is Temporary

The realization that everything in life is temporary became a profound lesson that shaped our perspective. It taught us to cherish each moment, for it will never come again. We learned to detach ourselves from the idea of permanence and embrace the acceptance of the ebb and flow of life. This understanding enabled us to let go of attachments and expectations, freeing ourselves to fully experience the beauty and transience of each passing moment.

Step 7: Mindfulness, Accepting Reality, & Gratitude

Mindfulness became the key that unlocked the door to a more fulfilling and meaningful life. By bringing our attention to the present moment, we learned to savor the richness of each experience. We cultivated an attitude of acceptance, embracing reality with open arms and finding peace in the midst of life's inevitable challenges. And through it all, gratitude became our constant companion— an ever-present reminder to appreciate the abundance that surrounds us. With each breath, we can express our heartfelt appreciation for the simple joys, the profound connections, and the gift of being alive. We say goodbye to life as it should be and embrace life as it is.

Let us continue this life-long journey. Let us remain committed to looking inward and striving to live our best lives. May the lessons and insights gained from this transformational process be a guiding light for others.

Embrace simplicity, declutter your mind, and cultivate gratitude for each precious moment. Share your stories, wisdom, and love with those around you. Be compassionate with yourself and those who temporarily cross your path. Leave behind an uncluttered legacy that will change the world.

May your life be filled with purpose, meaning, and a joy that knows no bounds. Your possibilities are endless.

Note from the Author

Thank you for embarking on this transformational journey with me. If you found this book informative, inspiring, or thought-provoking, I would be immensely grateful if you could take a moment to rate the book on Amazon.com.

Thank you! —Steven Todd Bryant

Printed in Great Britain
by Amazon